|THE FINAL CHAPTER

WHEN HEAVEN MEETS EARTH

Tom Stolz

www.bluedoorgeneration.com

|THE FINAL CHAPTER – WHEN HEAVEN MEETS EARTH

Generation Publishing, Portage, Michigan 49024

WWW.BLUEDOORGENERATION.COM

© 2016 Tom Stolz

Cover Photo: Sleeping Bear Dunes National Lakeshore (S. Stolz)
Edited By: Samantha Stolz

ISBN-13: 978-0692765487 (Generation Publishing)
ISBN-10: 0692765484

For Lonnie. Thanks for being obedient to Jesus to prophesy over me, and for all the support you have shown my family and I. Your heart to be a servant makes me want to be more like Jesus.

Table of Contents

Desiring Eden - 1

Worship is what transforms a city. Extravagantly giving myself in strength, thought, and emotion (heart, soul, and strength) in my words AND my actions is what will cause my physical geographic location to begin to reflect Eden.

Whether my mind knows it or not, my being (spirit, soul, and body) longs for Eden. A desire for Eden, which is an experience of being face to face with the One who knows me perfectly in a safe and life-filled place, is the quiet standard in my heart that is unsatisfied with the evil, or absence of God, that seems normal around me.

Psalms 63:1 O God, You are my God; Early will I seek You; My soul thirsts for You; My flesh longs for You In a dry and thirsty land Where there is no water.

Eden is True Life

Eden was what God called very good. Eden is what my heart was built to desire. My heart was made to be infinitely satisfied. I was made to live forever, therefore, I require an infinite source of satisfaction. Only an infinite well of transcendent, wonder-filled, love and beauty can satisfy the human heart. God is the only infinite well. Only God can satisfy my heart. Eden is the reality of me living satisfied, where God chose to physically dwell with man. This WILL be true forever, regardless of when I start really living like I believe it. I am supposed to long for true satisfaction

At the time Adam and Eve decided to doubt this reality, and fell, Eden was broken. For love, God erected a veil between His bright, holy, infinite, blazing, glory, and the darkened frame of man. Light destroys darkness, and until the darkness is worked out of my will, that blazing glory would harm me. Thanks to God, Jesus defeated the legal claim of darkness and became a gate, and a way, for me to walk in greater measures of light. God desires not for me to just "make it" through 80 physical years and then "see what happens next," but rather to, step by step, rejoin the supernatural realm (heaven), where He dwells, with my physical presence. This is the entire ideal of Eden, God with me, increasing in reality day by day, and this is the way to life as God defines it:

Matthew 7:13-14 "Enter by the narrow gate; for wide is the gate and broad is the way that leads to destruction, and there are many who go in by it. Because narrow is the gate and difficult is the way which leads to life, and there are few who find it.

A War Against Eden
There is a war against Eden. There is an enemy at work who desires to tempt me to feed on lesser pleasures...defining life simply in the physical realm... in order to dull my appetite for the superior pleasure, which is seeing more and more of the qualities of Eden appear in my life. The lie of the enemy to go after what the world says is good is a Satanic strategy to a) keep me from the gate, if possible, but then if Satan looses at plan a, to invoke plan b) keeping me from the "way" to Eden.

Many who name the name of Jesus have found the gate and, yet lost the way, believing God is mostly interested in their best life now. This strategy is straight from the devil who is a thief and a liar. This worldly thinking produces a cycle of physical longing (lust) and frustration as my hunger goes unsatisfied. As time goes on my search for satisfaction gets more frenzied...pulling me further and further from the infinite source of satisfaction who simply says "come to me and drink."

This cycle of lust and frustration which robs peace and satisfaction isn't limited to those in the "world." No! It is in the very Body of Jesus!

Thinking that doing things "for" Jesus protects me from this cycle is the greatest lie of all! Within ministries all over the Church, many measure their lives by the fulfillment of their desire to be successful as the world defines it: a "big" ministry, a "popular" book, the notice of a more famous leader (who is likely wishing someone more famous would notice them, too), accolades, recognition, a song or materials that sell, even just others to say "good word". This is all about getting a favorable evaluation from the physical, and making the actual increase of the supernatural secondary...The supernatural heavenly realm defines greatness much differently than the world:

Matthew 5:18-19 For assuredly, I say to you, till heaven and earth pass away, one jot or one tittle will by no means pass from the law till all is fulfilled. Whoever therefore breaks one of the least of these commandments, and teaches men so, shall be called least in the kingdom of heaven; but whoever does and teaches them, he shall be called great in the kingdom of heaven.

Jesus was the greatest teacher of the gospel the world has ever seen. He authored not just good songs, but music itself. Jesus wrote the Bible by the Spirit He sent into the world, lived the Sermon on the Mount better than anyone else, ever, and died with 12 guys following Him, who all ran away at just the wrong time. He died, from an earthly standard, very unsuccessfully, but He, as a man, completely recaptured Eden for the Father, restoring the possibility for what God calls "very good" for anyone else that wants to call that same thing very good. He IS the greatest forever...the name above all other names. If you want to live close to where He lives, you need to live close to like He lived!

Many who claim the name of Jesus think heaven will be good "someday", but for now are using their life to make "now" as good as possible. This is wrong thinking, through and through! God earnestly desires Eden NOW and is actively searching the earth for anyone to agree with Him that real life isn't even possible apart from Eden restored! To agree with Jesus in this is costly, but worth it.

II Chronicles 16:9 For the eyes of the Lord run to and fro throughout the whole earth, to show Himself strong on behalf of those whose heart is loyal to Him...

Life doesn't even start again until Eden is restored. That happens through the fire of tribulation which becomes a blaze in one generation. This passage, which Jesus said was an end-time passage, was written just for us:

Luke 12:49-53 "I came to send fire on the earth, and how I wish it were already kindled! But I have a baptism to be baptized with, and how

distressed I am till it is accomplished! Do you suppose that I came to give peace on earth? I tell you, not at all, but rather division. For from now on five in one house will be divided: three against two, and two against three. Father will be divided against son and son against father, mother against daughter and daughter against mother, mother-in-law against her daughter-in-law and daughter-in-law against her mother-in-law."

Jesus kindled this fire by the sacrifice of Himself and breathing the Spirit on those who would live intentionally for Eden. The wind of the Spirit has carried these embers to the ends of the earth and now, that kindling will become a blaze in the generation in which whole communities decide they will live for nothing less than Eden, NOW, not later!

II Peter 3:11-13 Therefore, since all these things will be dissolved, what manner of persons ought you to be in holy conduct and godliness, looking for and hastening the coming of the day of God, because of which the heavens will be dissolved, being on fire, and the elements will melt with fervent heat? Nevertheless we, according to His promise, look for new heavens and a new earth in which righteousness dwells.

The truth is we are supposed to be holding out for Eden. To get your best life now, in an environment less than Eden, is to have less life in the place intended to be "very good". This very common desire is totally out of synch with the leadership, and friendship, of Jesus:

Matthew 7:21-23 "Not everyone who says to Me, 'Lord, Lord,' shall enter the kingdom of heaven, but he who does the will of My Father in heaven. Many will say to Me in that day, 'Lord, Lord, have we not prophesied in Your name, cast out demons in Your name, and done many wonders in Your name?' And then I will declare to them, 'I never knew you; depart from Me, you who practice lawlessness!'

Stamping the name of Jesus on a worldly desire doesn't just drag me further from the superior pleasure of Eden, but it muddies the water for every other beloved one of the Father who comes after me.

Many are newly born of the Spirit and given a heart to look for the ideal of purity in their relationship with God and the power that flows from a bright and vibrant interaction with Him. To claim to know God, yet live desiring the world's values and rewards is to betray the very ideal Jesus paid for. Many have been deluded and harmed by this very dynamic in Jesus' Body. The world's ways can never draw me closer to the actual source of life. The world's ways might draw more people to me, but what good is it to win the world and loose my own fidelity to being with Jesus as the pinnacle of enjoyment...to lose my own fascination with His plans...my own reach for Eden?

Matthew 16:26 For what profit is it to a man if he gains the whole world, and loses his own soul? Or what will a man give in exchange for his soul?

It's All About Desire

It is a question of worship. Worship is the highest expression of desire. We were made to live in Eden and worship the greatest thing we could see, the bright holiness of God, our never ending source of life. Since the moment Eden was broken, and the veil erected...since man was separated from seeing God...we have had to fight our eyes from worshiping the choice things of the broken world. Worship is the first step in choosing our strength. We all have to choose what we define as strength...what we define as success. We choose the strength of our lives with our trust, with our faith. Whichever strength we choose is the one that manifests in our life...it is what we stand on:

Matthew 7:24-27 "Therefore whoever hears these sayings of Mine, and does them, I will liken him to a wise man who built his house on the rock: and the rain descended, the floods came, and the winds blew and beat on that house; and it did not fall, for it was founded on the rock. "But everyone who hears these sayings of Mine, and does not do them, will be like a foolish man who built his house on the sand: and the rain descended, the floods came, and the winds blew and beat on that house; and it fell. And great was its fall."

Luke 18:1-2, 6-8 THEN He spoke a parable to them, that men always ought to pray and not lose heart, saying: "There was in a certain city a judge who did not fear God nor regard man.... Then the Lord said,

"Hear what the unjust judge said. And shall God not avenge His own elect who cry out day and night to Him, though He bears long with them? I tell you that He will avenge them speedily. Nevertheless, when the Son of Man comes, will He really find faith on the earth?"

The "then" in vs. 1 follows the last thing Jesus taught in Chapter 17 of Luke. Luke 17 is the equivalent of Matthew 24...this is Jesus teaching about the last 7 years leading up to His physical return to re-establish Eden over 1,000 years.

He finishes off the teaching by prophesying that God will respond to the night and day cry of His people. 24-hour worship and prayer is one of the most-prophesied aspects of the end-times. Right now, over hundreds, if not thousands, of locations are contending for night and day worship...this is one of the most blatantly obvious signs of the times pointing to the soon-return of Jesus, but so few know about it!!

24-hour worship seems like a new thing to many people, but it is actually the most Biblical way to worship. It is one of the oldest ways to worship corporately. This is what David's Tabernacle was all about. David hired 4,000 singers and musicians to keep night and day worship going in Jerusalem. This was eventually moved into a permanent location, called the Temple. God took this very seriously. Most of the Book of Psalms was written in less than 40 years by David and his night and day singers. Solomon's Temple, and its 24-hour worship format was ALL about responding to God's desire for "very good," or God's desire to be with His people face to face. God promised Solomon that if He took the Temple seriously like His dad did, then God would dwell in the land with them:

I Kings 6:11-14 Then the word of the Lord came to Solomon, saying: " Concerning this temple which you are building, if you walk in My statutes, execute My judgments, keep all My commandments, and walk in them, then I will perform My word with you, which I spoke to your father David. And I will dwell among the children of Israel, and will not forsake My people Israel." So Solomon built the temple and finished it.

The Tabernacle Desire Expressed

The temple, or tabernacle...24 hour worship and prayer... Was the qualifying reality for the presence of God. Continual desire for God results in the continuous manifestation of His presence. Because God gave earth to mankind to dominate, God honors what it is man desires. Where man desires self gratification, what they get is what man can self-produce...death, war, famine...

But, in geographic locations where man desires God, what a community can expect is all that God can produce in the life mankind. A restored Eden is just the beginning!

Worship is the highest expression of desire. God searches the earth looking for people that desire what He desires (people who are loyal to Him and His plan to restore the earth back to Eden) and then He gives them faith to start changing the land back to Eden, step by step. This is what the Temple was all about. By the time Solomon's reign was established, the land of Israel had started to physically change:

II Chronicles 9:22-27 So King Solomon surpassed all the kings of the earth in riches and wisdom. And all the kings of the earth sought the presence of Solomon to hear his wisdom, which God had put in his heart. Each man brought his present: articles of silver and gold, garments, armor, spices, horses, and mules, at a set rate year by year. Solomon had four thousand stalls for horses and chariots, and twelve thousand horsemen whom he stationed in the chariot cities and with the king at Jerusalem. So he reigned over all the kings from the River to the land of the Philistines, as far as the border of Egypt. The king made silver as common in Jerusalem as stones, and he made cedar trees as abundant as the sycamores which are in the lowland.

How did a man make cedars as common as sycamores? By putting His faith in God and leading the people in making worship and prayer THE priority in the geographic region he was responsible for. Even the military leaders were connected to the Temple. God responded by filling Solomon's mind with wisdom and insight, changing the nature of the economy, protecting the land from enemies, and changing the very nature of...nature! This is the promise God has always held out to His people willing to agree with Him:

Leviticus 26:3-12 'If you walk in My statutes and keep My commandments, and perform them, then I will give you rain in its season, the land shall yield its produce, and the trees of the field shall yield their fruit. Your threshing shall last till the time of vintage...and dwell in your land safely. I will give peace in the land, and you shall lie down, and none will make you afraid; I will rid the land of evil beasts, and the sword will not go through your land. You will chase your enemies... your enemies shall fall by the sword before you. 'For I will look on you favorably and make you fruitful, multiply you and confirm My covenant with you...I will set My tabernacle among you, and My soul shall not abhor you. I will walk among you and be your God, and you shall be My people.

Desire Transforms Our World

This is the beginning, and the point of, Eden: a lush place to live for man and God to dwell together.

Getting back to Eden begins with worship and ends with the transformation of the land. This is why: because FAITH transforms the physical realm to agree with heaven, where God is. God has given the earth to mankind, which means we really have a say in the quality of our land, economy, and the extent to which we encounter God. According to the Bible, this all comes down to how we approach God in worship. Do we dwell together in worship as a united family who's number one goal is agreeing with God about what happens around His throne? Do we make a night and day cry out to Him our actual strength? Or do we make other earthly things our strength and do worship when it is convenient for us, or elevates us? This is really the question!

24-hour worship is probably one of the MOST INCONVENIENT THINGS THE CHURCH CAN DO!! BY DESIGN. It requires putting aside other permissible things in order to "keep the fire on the altar." To maintain 24-hour worship, you have to REALLY believe God is the only answer, source, and reward. Otherwise, you will quit. Behind every 24-hour worship location, there are at least a few "crazy" people who are giving their ENTIRE lives to it or else it would simply stop. You can't sustain 24-hour worship half-heartedly...it is impossible, by design. This is the first commandment:

Matthew 22:35-40 Then one of them, a lawyer, asked Him a question, testing Him, and saying, "Teacher, which is the great commandment in the law?" Jesus said to him, " 'You shall love the Lord your God with all your heart, with all your soul, and with all your mind.' This is the first and great commandment. And the second is like it: 'You shall love your neighbor as yourself.' On these two commandments hang all the Law and the Prophets."

The temple worship order required both commandments be held to in order to work. 24-hour worship with a bunch of people is the context of living out Jesus' two most important commandments! That is why He was so disgusted with what the Temple had become at the time of His first coming. This is why He threw over the tables and declared "this place is supposed to be a House of Prayer!"

Yes, the temple was "open" 24-hours a day, but at the time of Jesus' first coming, most people didn't see the worship 24/7 as their priority in life. One person named Anna did, and she was a forerunner to Jesus coming the first time. Anna was the only one recorded that was longing for Eden in the Temple day and night:

Luke 2:36-38 Now there was one, Anna, a prophetess, the daughter of Phanuel, of the tribe of Asher. She was of a great age, and had lived with a husband seven years from her virginity; and this woman was a widow of about eighty-four years, who did not depart from the temple, but served God with fastings and prayers night and day. And coming in that instant she gave thanks to the Lord, and spoke of Him to all those who looked for redemption in Jerusalem.

Anna had faith to remain in the Temple expressing her desire to God for the Messiah. Anna got what she contended for, which was the biggest step back to Eden mankind has taken, to date. Jesus made the very return to Eden possible, and God made a point of letting the world know that Anna was the one with a night and day presence in the Temple contending for it.

Faith changes the physical realm to move back in the direction of Eden, because faith is the conscious act of "putting all your eggs" in the basket of God's presence:

Matthew 21:18-22 Now in the morning, as He returned to the city, He was hungry. And seeing a fig tree by the road, He came to it and found nothing on it but leaves, and said to it, "Let no fruit grow on you ever again." Immediately the fig tree withered away. And when the disciples saw it, they marveled, saying, "How did the fig tree wither away so soon?" So Jesus answered and said to them, "Assuredly, I say to you, if you have faith and do not doubt, you will not only do what was done to the fig tree, but also if you say to this mountain, 'Be removed and be cast into the sea,' it will be done. And whatever things you ask in prayer, believing, you will receive."

Unlimited Desire

Faith changes the physical realm to agree with heaven. BUT, most people don't have mountain-moving faith. What all people have is unlimited desire. Desire is the currency of heaven. You spend it with your words. The temple was the place to express desire in worship. That worship, expressing desire in the highest possible way, obtains earth changing faith.

The passage from Matthew above isn't symbolic. The tree really died. We are supposed to speak to the physical and see it change. But, this is a process of dying to ourselves, taking up the cause of Eden wholeheartedly, and step by step growing into this faith. This starts globally with 24-hour worship at the time immediately preceding Jesus' return.

There is a VERY specific reason Jesus prophesied night and day prayer will precede His return. God is searching the earth right now to find all those longing for Eden...all those willing to trade a broken life here and now and earnestly DESIRE to live with God where He is. This is what David desired. This is why God showed him how to do night and day worship, just as it happens around God's throne. This was David's heart-desire:

Psalms 27:4-5 One thing I have desired of the Lord , That will I seek: That I may dwell in the house of the Lord All the days of my life, To behold the beauty of the Lord , And to inquire in His temple. For in the time of trouble He shall hide me in His pavilion; In the secret place of His tabernacle He shall hide me; He shall set me high upon a rock.

David said "I want Eden, God! I want you and me, face to face, that is the only safe place." God showed David how to be with Him more and more, by showing him how to agree on earth with the way desire is expressed night and day in Heaven.

Revelation 4:8-10 The four living creatures, each having six wings, were full of eyes around and within. And they do not rest day or night, saying: "Holy, holy, holy, Lord God Almighty, Who was and is and is to come!" Whenever the living creatures give glory and honor and thanks to Him who sits on the throne, who lives forever and ever, the twenty-four elders fall down before Him who sits on the throne and worship Him who lives forever and ever, and cast their crowns before the throne, saying:

Day and night, night and day, those closest to God, the Seraphim, continually catch glimpses of His blazing beauty, which is pure love, power, mercy...every good thing and desire...continually welling up from God's presence. The Seraphim desire more and more of this insight. God is truly the most glorious sight to behold, and the Seraphim remain before God night and day, not because it is their job, but because they are allowed to, it is their desire. They are the burning ones, literally consumed with the fire of His presence, but more alive than any other created thing. They are called "the living creatures." Think burning bush: alive, but consumed in glorious holy fire.

God showed David how to begin releasing the glory of what the Seraphim see, but right here on earth! This is how heaven will come to earth: by mankind getting glimpses of it and WANTING it. The first glimpses are captured by hearing and responding.

Prophetically, the musicians and singers in David's tabernacle gazed, ever so dimly, on this same transcendent beauty and declared it into the tent David set up, which later moved to the earthly temple. This changed the land. This, David said, would create a safe place in a "time of trouble."

The Tabernacle has always been for a time of trouble. Amos, Jesus, Joel, John the beloved, Isaiah, Jeremiah, Zechariah...I could even go on...these men all prophesied a God-designed time of trouble that is allowed to get all men to choose the same thing Joshua chose: whom they will serve!

Choosing Life

Whoever desires Eden...to live in the presence of the Lord...will get what they want, just like David. Whoever desires to live absent God will get what they want, too. To chooses existence without God...an attempt at life where God isn't...is to choose a barren lake of fire.

God owns creation. He is the light source of creation. The sun pales in comparison. You literally cannot live apart from God's glory, but all who choose to attempt it will be allowed to try. For the sake of love God will not violate free will. But, the TRUTH is, you cannot live apart from the light of man any more than a tree can live apart from the sun:

John 1:3-5 All things were made through Him, and without Him nothing was made that was made. In Him was life, and the life was the light of men. And the light shines in the darkness, and the darkness did not comprehend it.

So this is the plan: in one generation God will give everyone, incrementally, what they want. A large group want man-based security. They want the tangible plan of a man to make them safe, sound, rich, and happy. One generation will want to cast off the restraints of God's moral ways and do what feels right more than any other before it. This final generation before Jesus will want their best life NOW! They will be given what they want, which is really evil, or the absence of God. God will lift His "hand of restraint" currently protecting mankind from itself, and hand this generation what it desires, globally. The antichrist will be given 3.5 years to show this lawless generation what he is really all about, just like Jesus took 3.5 years to show the earth what is in His heart. The anti-Jesus, a humanistic "messiah", is evil because he desires to replace God with himself, and to save people through his intellect and earthly talents. What will result is the same thing that always happens when large groups of people trust a man to make the earth fair: war, famine, death, and a few elites controlling most of the resources. This is a time of trouble.

David and Jesus said the night and day prayer movement IS for such a time of trouble! God has a plan to start giving Eden, bit by bit, to anyone willing to die to the idea of their best life now, and trade it for a desire for Eden, which is what God desires, and what David desired.

Amos 9:9-12 "For I will give the command and will shake Israel along with the other nations as grain is shaken in a sieve, yet not one true kernel will be lost. But all the sinners will die by the sword— all those who say, 'Nothing bad will happen to us.' "In that day I will restore the fallen house of David. I will repair its damaged walls. From the ruins I will rebuild it and restore its former glory. And Israel will possess what is left of Edom and all the nations I have called to be mine. " The Lord has spoken, and he will do these things.

Spending Desire Purchases Faith

Amos prophesied that temple worship locations (the tabernacle of David) will be raised up in all the nations, to allow the shaking of all the nations to be done without losing the true grains (think wheat and tares). This is God's plan to protect all those longing for Eden: to give them the plans, just like He gave David, to express their desire day and night. This will result in the release of earth-changing faith, also called the "pouring out of the Spirit."

Faith is a fruit of the Spirit. The pouring out of the Spirit in response to "desire expressed" will result in faith to change the physical realm, as well as hope, love, patience, peace, gentleness, self control, goodness...in the midst of the rest of the earth maturing in evil. Pockets of "Eden-longers" will start getting Eden, as the Spirit is poured out. This is what the Book of Revelation is all about: Eden-longers progressively getting more and more tastes of Eden, and then expressing more and more desire for Eden in a cycle that transforms their land, and purifies entire communities...preparing all who want to be with God to be married to His son. Agreeing with heaven's order in the tabernacle will prepare God's children to become legal sons and daughters to rule the earth and possess the inheritance of the Son, and make themselves ready for the wedding by expressing desire night and day and seeing heaven open in their city of refuge.

Revelation 7 describes a multitude without number watching this take place, coming out of the world system which is crumbling all around as the world is given what it wants, and these lands of refuge...tabernacle locations, swelling with people. God has a plan to protect all those who agree with Him, as He has every other time judgment has been released. His plan is for a multitude without number to come in out of the cold dying world, where the very land itself is being given over to the curse mankind is choosing, into the night and day worshiping places:

Revelation 7:9-17 After these things I looked, and behold, a great multitude which no one could number, of all nations, tribes, peoples, and tongues, standing before the throne and before the Lamb, clothed with white robes, with palm branches in their hands, and crying out with a loud voice, saying, "Salvation belongs to our God who sits on the throne, and to the Lamb!" All the angels stood around the throne and the elders and the four living creatures, and fell on their faces before the throne and worshiped God, saying: "Amen! Blessing and glory and wisdom, Thanksgiving and honor and power and might, Be to our God forever and ever. Amen." Then one of the elders answered, saying to me, "Who are these arrayed in white robes, and where did they come from?" And I said to him, "Sir, you know." So he said to me, "These are the ones who come out of the great tribulation, and washed their robes and made them white in the blood of the Lamb. Therefore they are before the throne of God (in the Spirit, just like we are now)*, and serve Him day and night in His temple* (they have come into agreement with David and God about how to long for Eden). *And He who sits on the throne will dwell among them* (and they will get what they want, God with mankind, note that the word "will" indicates this will happen in the future). *They shall neither hunger anymore nor thirst anymore* (the rest of the world is in famine)*; the sun shall not strike them* (this is one of the trumpet judgments), nor any heat (bowl judgment)*; for the Lamb who is in the midst of the throne will shepherd them and lead them to living fountains of waters* (He will guide them to every resource they need)*. And God will wipe away every tear from their eyes* (they will not sorrow in the midst of the most sorrowful time the earth has ever seen)*."*

This is God's plan to make a difference between all those who desire Eden and those who don't, so that as mankind witnesses it, all who want God will repent and come into agreement with Him. The oldest way of expressing desire, the pattern God gave to David, the man after His own heart, is coming back into style as a means to save cities, and multitudes without number!

The Falling Away - 2

Because God has given dominion of the earth to mankind, our choices have massive implications. Our desire expressed in the earth effects change in not only the geography around us, but also the desires of others around us. The fire in our heart is "catching," like the burning bush Moses encountered in the desert, the fire of God consumes AND brings life.

For this reason, the longing for Eden expressed in one generation will not be neutral. This singular desire expressed in a company of people will get Jesus a pure and spotless Bride, but it will simultaneously produce offense in those NOT longing for Eden. Many in the Church will fall away as the dark powers of the earth resist those growing in lovesick desire for Eden to be re-established:

II Thessalonians 2:1-6 Now, brethren, concerning the coming of our Lord Jesus Christ and our gathering together to Him, we ask you, not to be soon shaken in mind or troubled, either by spirit or by word or by letter, as if from us, as though the day of Christ had come. Let no one deceive you by any means; for that Day will not come unless the falling away comes first, and the man of sin is revealed, the son of perdition, who opposes and exalts himself above all that is called God or that is worshiped, so that he sits as God in the temple of God, showing himself that he is God. Do you not remember that when I was still with you I told you these things? And now you know what is restraining, that he may be revealed in his own time.

We live in the time of the increase in lawlessness and the great "falling away." The falling away is a mostly misunderstood topic. It is a topic that is offensive to the Church. No one wants to believe that THEY could fall away. If you think you could not fall away, you are actually a prime candidate TO fall away...for real. Only pride would cause someone to think a warning Jesus gave his disciples did not apply to them, too!

Proverbs 16:18 Pride goes before destruction, And a haughty spirit before a fall.

Falling away means to "quit being a Christian in a time of tribulation." This is a clear doctrine of Jesus and the disciples. In the parable of the sower, Jesus taught directly on the nature of falling away:

Luke 8:13 But the ones on the rock are those who, when they hear, receive the word with joy; and these have no root, who believe for a while and in time of temptation fall away.

Falling away is permanent:

Hebrews 6:4-6 For it is impossible for those who were once enlightened, and have tasted the heavenly gift, and have become partakers of the Holy Spirit, and have tasted the good word of God and the powers of the age to come, if they fall away, to renew them again to repentance, since they crucify again for themselves the Son of God, and put Him to an open shame.

Offense Produces the Falling Away

The falling away in the last days will result from believers who have no root in the Sermon on the Mount deciding to take the mark of the beast and betray other Christians to save their own skin. The truth of who the antichrist is, and his opposition to Jesus, when spoken of by those loyal to Jesus, is going to result in Christians being hated "in every nation." It will be illegal to be a Christian in every nation, just as it is in many nations already. When the fullness of this time comes...I believe in years, not decades...governments of the earth will begin aligning with the politically correct elements of Jesus' body. I believe, just as has happened in the past, many governments of the earth will say "fundamentalist Christians are traitors and subvertors. Either you are with the good things the government is trying to do, or you are with them. If you are with the fundamentalists, you will be punished like them." Those who don't fall in line with the government will be persecuted. This dynamic will create an atmosphere of betrayal within the Church.

False teachers know what to teach to keep people listening. In order to give comfort to compromisers, they will encourage watering down the truth in the name of "unity." Both loyal followers of Jesus, and false teachers, are talking about unity in this hour. Utter confusion is the result. Not all unity is Jesus-based. True God-pleasing unity is based on unwavering loyalty to truth. False unity bases unity on man-based logic. Only truth will "endure."

When warning His disciples about the "last days" leading to His return, Jesus warned His disciples PRIVATELY about the exact conditions that would produce the falling away Paul warned of in the 2 Thessalonians passage I quoted at the beginning:

Matthew 24:9-14 "Then they will deliver you up to tribulation and kill you, and you will be hated by all nations for My name's sake. And then many will be offended, will betray one another, and will hate one another. Then many false prophets will rise up and deceive many. And because lawlessness will abound, the love of many will grow cold. But he who endures to the end shall be saved. And this gospel of the kingdom will be preached in all the world as a witness to all the nations, and then the end will come.

False Teachers Will Fuel the Falling Away

Jesus, Paul, Peter, James, Jude, and John all warned of the danger of falling away due to tribulation, offense, and false teachers in the last days. In our day very few want to talk about tribulation, almost no one talks anymore about being offended with Jesus' intense end time plans, and false teachers roam about mostly unchecked in Jesus' body at this moment. These are the EXACT conditions the gospels and the epistles warn of. A perfect storm will emerge, according to Jesus in Matthew 7. You need a solid foundation to endure the end time storm.

Right now, there are many false teachers and prophets in the mainstream body of Christ. They are increasing in number. They don't set out to be false teachers, but they become false teachers because they let the fear of the opinions of other people drive them more than God. They believe the world's economy is more real than God's invisible economy. They might teach about self-denial in shallow ways, but they don't deny themselves houses, cars, influence, or opportunity. False teachers are easy to spot once you get the Biblical paradigm, but many are very popular teachers. There is an element of power and anointing in the ministry of modern false teachers.

Jesus warned that it is the fruit of a teacher's life and teaching that we use to judge a teacher, not the power in their ministry or the sound of their words. Those that are loyal to Jesus must say things that are offensive to darkness, and EVERYONE has some measure of darkness they need to deal with. A true teacher doesn't say things to avoid disturbing the dark places...in loyalty to the Light of Mankind, they shine light to illuminate the dark places. Light offends darkness. For this reason, we cannot judge teachers by how good they leave us feeling, but rather we judge by how much they encourage us to love Jesus at cost! Obedience at cost is the bond of true unity in Jesus' end-time Bride.

According to Jesus, it is what the message produces that matters. The two fruits that must be produced by messages that agree with God are these: 1. A wholehearted zeal to love God. 2. A love for God that overflows into genuine love for others.

Jesus warned that many would teach and do seemingly great things in Jesus' name, but they would be driven by motivations other than loyalty to Jesus and His true message that offends darkness. False teachers value life now more than the vision of life in Jesus' presence on earth. They, and those that follow them, will be shut out in the time of Jesus' appearing:

Matthew 7:21-23 "Not everyone who says to Me, 'Lord, Lord,' shall enter the kingdom of heaven, but he who does the will of My Father in heaven. Many will say to Me in that day, 'Lord, Lord, have we not prophesied in Your name, cast out demons in Your name, and done many wonders in Your name?' And then I will declare to them, 'I never knew you; depart from Me, you who practice lawlessness!'

"Lawlessness" means operating outside of obedience to Jesus. Obeying Jesus often offends people. False teachers get their standing from people rather than Jesus, reaching to those "leaders" greater than themselves with hope of being elevated, and eating up those lower than themselves, feeding on the loyalty and the resources of those they consider "the people." In the Bible there are not two classes of Christians. There is the 1 Corinthians 12 "body." A true teacher encourages EVERYONE to lead in their area of authority, paying more honor to those who seem less honorable.

The world trades power for loyalty, but God gives freely. God values humility. Truly great teachers serve people...not just teaching, but doing the things they tell others they should do! If you want to be great, you must teach AND do:

Matthew 5:19 Whoever therefore breaks one of the least of these commandments, and teaches men so, shall be called least in the kingdom of heaven; but whoever does and teaches them, he shall be called great in the kingdom of heaven.

Loyalty to Jesus' Leadership Will Be Tested

True followers of Jesus must be discerning. You must judge the fruit of those you receive from. What does their teaching produce in their life? What does it produce in your heart? I don't want Bible verses that encourage me to be comfortable where I am. I want to hear teaching that drives me to love Jesus and others more. Loving people is telling them the truth, and the truth is we need to want to be more like Jesus.

"Group think" is leading many astray. The Bible warns of this over and over. When people take the easy route of falling in with all the other people, rather than do the hard work of thinking for themselves, the whole group goes down together. Psalm 14 deals directly with this aspect of the end times:

Psalms 14:3-6 They have all turned aside, They have together become corrupt; There is none who does good, No, not one. Have all the workers of iniquity no knowledge, Who eat up my people as they eat bread, And do not call on the Lord ? There they are in great fear, For God is with the generation of the righteous. You shame the counsel of the poor, But the Lord is his refuge.

In this Psalm, David is talking about the collective group of people who listen to each other, rather than to the unpopular messages of warning from God. God is preparing the earth for judgment, and "the group" is saying God is doing something entirely different. But hiding from the truth doesn't change the truth. The result is always the same: fear grows in the group as the intense light of truth grows brighter. The "poor", or unpopular, one who stands for truth is often an outsider.

The Psalmist says "no one listens to the little guy everyone is shunning, but don't you know He couldn't stand if God weren't standing with him?!" The little guy would cave in to peer pressure if it weren't for God. The group that worries what others think stands in the light of each other, but the lone voice of warning stands with God.

Take heed, Church, Psalm 14 warns the group that "great fear" is coming when the truth of judgment dawns brighter. The intensity of truth is increasing in this very hour! There are numerous warnings in the Bible about prophets who promise peace when trouble is coming. There is not one warning in the Bible about prophets who warn of trouble when peace is coming!

There is a testing of the heart everyone who walks in fidelity with Jesus must endure to see what their internal motivation is. David spoke of this often, and so did Jesus. Mankind judges by outward appearance, but God tests the heart. People tend to think that if a person is popular, he or she is correct. This is exactly the opposite of the way the kingdom works! Jesus, the greatest preacher of the gospel ever, only had 12 guys with Him by the time He was done delivering the full gospel!

John 6:56-68 He who eats My flesh and drinks My blood abides in Me, and I in him. As the living Father sent Me, and I live because of the Father, so he who feeds on Me will live because of Me. This is the bread which came down from heaven—not as your fathers ate the manna, and are dead. He who eats this bread will live forever." These things He said in the synagogue as He taught in Capernaum. Therefore many of His disciples, when they heard this, said, "This is a hard saying; who can understand it?" When Jesus knew in Himself that His disciples complained about this, He said to them, "Does this offend you? What then if you should see the Son of Man ascend where He was before? It is the Spirit who gives life; the flesh profits nothing. The words that I speak to you are spirit, and they are life. But there are some of you who do not believe." For Jesus knew from the beginning who they were who did not believe, and who would betray Him. And He said, "Therefore I have said to you that no one can come to Me unless it has been granted to him by My Father." From that time many of His disciples went back and walked with Him no more. Then Jesus said to the twelve, "Do you also want to go away?" But Simon Peter answered Him, "Lord, to whom shall we go? You have the words of eternal life.

Jesus is coming to take over the leadership of the earth!

The true message of Jesus is OFFENSIVE to the fallen heart of man. The gospel message manifesting as the government of the earth...the light coming into the darkness in the last years...is EVEN MORE OFFENSIVE. Jesus warned His disciples that the offense of His message and the reaction it would produce would only get worse, not better, in the last days:

Luke 23:28-31 But Jesus, turning to them, said, "Daughters of Jerusalem, do not weep for Me, but weep for yourselves and for your children. For indeed the days are coming in which they will say, 'Blessed are the barren, wombs that never bore, and breasts which never nursed!' Then they will begin 'to say to the mountains, "Fall on us!" and to the hills, "Cover us!" ' For if they do these things in the green wood, what will be done in the dry?"

Jesus said this while He was hanging on a cross for demonstrating the true nature of love! He told His disciples to expect the exact same treatment He received:

John 15:18-23 "If the world hates you, you know that it hated Me before it hated you. If you were of the world, the world would love its own. Yet because you are not of the world, but I chose you out of the world, therefore the world hates you. Remember the word that I said to you, 'A servant is not greater than his master.' If they persecuted Me, they will also persecute you. If they kept My word, they will keep yours also. But all these things they will do to you for My name's sake, because they do not know Him who sent Me. If I had not come and spoken to them, they would have no sin, but now they have no excuse for their sin. He who hates Me hates My Father also.

We Must Learn to Stand

In order to endure this time of truth emerging in darkness, we need to be ready to stand, even when everyone we know is telling us to back down. This starts small and grows. Jesus promised it would start with churches and then go up the food chain, into governmental authorities. The ones who haul you before "synagogues" because they worry about how your message makes the church look are the same ones who, if they refuse to repent, will turn loyal fundamental Christians over to authorities when their own livelihood in the church is threatened by the government.

Everyone must stand for truth now or later. Now is the time to train your heart to stand. If you wait, it only gets more dangerous for everyone as those who fear men continue to betray the true messages of warning. Faith and loyalty get stronger with use. Anyone who stands for truth will be made ready to stand more, and anyone who falls in the small beginnings of tribulation will fall away when the pressure increases, unless they repent and learn to stand. You owe it to Jesus to speak truth to them. This helps you AND the leader who is stumbling in weakness. Now is the time to find out what Jesus is doing in this hour and get ready to endure!

Mark 13:8-13 For nation will rise against nation, and kingdom against kingdom. And there will be earthquakes in various places, and there will be famines and troubles. These are the beginnings of sorrows. "But watch out for yourselves, for they will deliver you up to councils, and you will be beaten in the synagogues. You will be brought before rulers and kings for My sake, for a testimony to them. And the gospel must first be preached to all the nations. But when they arrest you and deliver you up, do not worry beforehand, or premeditate what you will speak. But whatever is given you in that hour, speak that; for it is not you who speak, but the Holy Spirit. Now brother will betray brother to death, and a father his child; and children will rise up against parents and cause them to be put to death. And you will be hated by all for My name's sake. But he who endures to the end shall be saved.

Knowing the Plan Prevents Offense
One of the greatest lies to have been foisted on the believers in our generation is that the return of Jesus will occur at any minute, that no one could know when that minute is, and that there is nothing to be done but do your best and wait to be sucked up into the sky. This is so far from the action plan Jesus left for His disciples. In fact, it is a Satanic setup to produce a great falling away that will steal many from the harvest God desires.

Not knowing or participating in what Jesus is doing in this hour, when the intensity increases to a level no one has ever seen, will create great offense in those who think they know Jesus. This offense, according to the Bible, will cause many to go with the rest of the world in rebellion because they are afraid of the consequences of staying loyal to Jesus. Jesus gave very clear instruction to His disciples regarding how to hasten the intense Day of the Lord (pray), what to watch for to mark the progress of the intense Day of the Lord (watch) , and how to prepare for the intense Day of the Lord (be ready).

Watch. Pray. Be Ready
Every time Jesus spoke of His return, He admonished His disciples to watch, pray, and/or be ready. There are very specific things we MUST do to participate with Jesus in His return. To be able to do those things in obedience and agreement with our King's BRILLIANT plan, we must know the plan and watch for the signs. Just like a farmer plants in the spring and harvests in the fall, certain actions are required in different seasons. We are supposed to know the season we are in! Listen to this end time statement God made through Isaiah:

Isaiah 28:21-29 (GNT) The Lord will fight as he did at Mount Perazim and in the valley of Gibeon, in order to do what he intends to do— strange as his actions may seem. He will complete his work, his mysterious work. Don't laugh at the warning I am giving you! If you do, it will be even harder for you to escape. I have heard the Lord Almighty's decision to destroy the whole country. Listen to what I am saying; pay attention to what I am telling you. Farmers don't constantly plow their fields and keep getting them ready for planting. Once they have prepared the soil, they plant the seeds of herbs such as dill and cumin. They plant rows of wheat and barley, and at the edges of their fields they plant other grain. They know how to do their work,

because God has taught them. They never use a heavy club to beat out
dill seeds or cumin seeds; instead they use light sticks of the proper
size. They do not ruin the wheat by threshing it endlessly, and they
know how to thresh it by driving a cart over it without bruising the
grains. All this wisdom comes from the Lord Almighty. The plans God
makes are wise, and they always succeed.

Knowing the plan and the intensity we are supposed to be getting ready for prevents the Bride from being offended when things get hot! The greatest preventative for falling away is knowing, and being realistic about, what to expect.

I have taught Revelation for a few years. What I find from teaching it is that people who come into Revelation afraid (once they understand God's plan) go out from Revelation confident and excited about the time they live in, but it takes an intentional study of the information. God has very intense plans promised! Not every earthquake is a "bad" earthquake. There are specific things to pray for in specific ways. Once you see them and participate in them, confidence builds for what is next! Our Father, who requires our loyalty to His judgments, has some pretty rough stuff in store. We need to know when and why He is doing what He is doing so we can declare things in agreement with Him and grow in oneness with Him! That is the point of Revelation. It is the story of our wedding!

There are over 150 Chapters in the Bible dedicated to describing the final generation on earth that will witness the return of Jesus. The Bible is actually mostly about our generation! The Bible has significantly more information regarding Jesus' return than it does regarding His first coming. There are 89 chapters that comprise the Gospels, several of which primarily describe events related to Jesus return, while there are over 150 Chapters throughout the Bible that primarily describe Jesus' return. There is no lack of information to digest to be equipped to understand exactly what God is doing, when He is doing it, and WHY He is doing it in our generation, yet Revelation is one of the least understood Books in the Bible. This is a strategic deception the enemy is implementing in order to maximize the falling away.

The Reward of Doing Revelation

Teaching Revelation comes at great cost. Many existing leaders in Jesus' body actually oppose the simple teaching of Revelation! That is why Revelation is one of two places that promise a blessing for reading and keeping (or making choices that agree with) the book. The other place in the Bible that promises a blessing for doing and teaching the contents is the Sermon on the Mount (Matthew 5,6, and 7), which promises greatness to those who do and teach it!

Revelation 1:1-3 The Revelation of Jesus Christ, which God gave Him to show His servants—things which must shortly take place. And He sent and signified it by His angel to His servant John, who bore witness to the word of God, and to the testimony of Jesus Christ, to all things that he saw. Blessed is he who reads and those who hear the words of this prophecy, and keep those things which are written in it; for the time is near.

Matthew 5:18-20 For assuredly, I say to you, till heaven and earth pass away, one jot or one tittle will by no means pass from the law till all is fulfilled. Whoever therefore breaks one of the least of these commandments, and teaches men so, shall be called least in the kingdom of heaven; but whoever does and teaches them, he shall be called great in the kingdom of heaven. For I say to you, that unless your righteousness exceeds the righteousness of the scribes and Pharisees, you will by no means enter the kingdom of heaven.

The reason that this promise is found in these two places is that Revelation and the Sermon on the Mount are divinely connected to each other. Revelation is the motivation to do the Sermon on the Mount, because the Sermon on the Mount is the antidote to the trouble that will touch the earth through the events described in Revelation!

Wherever Revelation is taught in its main and plain meaning, the fruit is always the same: an increased focus and desire to prepare for the intense events by following the roadmap in the Sermon on the Mount to wholehearted zealous love for Jesus.

This process ruins a person for this world. If you want to be ready for heaven to come to earth, you have to train your heart to let go of your desire for earth without heaven. This is what the Sermon on the Mount is all about. This re-training of the heart takes time. This is what it means to "store oil" like Jesus described in the Parable of the 10

Bridesmaids (Matthew 25). Storing oil happens in advance of when you need it! You need to take time in advance to store up oil to make it through the darkest part of earth's natural history.

The Great and Terrible Conclusion

Jesus' first coming was a "down payment" on the fullness of the prophecies of the coming of the Messiah to deliver the earth out of darkness and back into the face to face presence of God. The entire Bible is the story of the process God has chosen to restore everything that was lost in the fall of man in Genesis 3.

God made the earth to be a dwelling place where He could meet face to face with His beloved family of mankind. THAT is what God called "very good" in Genesis 1:31, and that is what He is in the process of restoring. The climax of the story happens in the final 7 years leading up to the return of Jesus. We call that final seven year period the "tribulation" and the second half of the final seven years, 1,260 days to be exact, we call the "Great Tribulation." The tribulation, which turns into the Great Tribulation, will be the hardest time the earth has ever witnessed, but it will also be the greatest time to be alive if you are ready for it! Listen to what Daniel was told about the Great Tribulation:

Daniel 12:1-4 "At that time Michael shall stand up, The great prince who stands watch over the sons of your people; And there shall be a time of trouble, Such as never was since there was a nation, Even to that time. And at that time your people shall be delivered, Every one who is found written in the book. And many of those who sleep in the dust of the earth shall awake, Some to everlasting life, Some to shame and everlasting contempt. Those who are wise shall shine Like the brightness of the firmament, And those who turn many to righteousness Like the stars forever and ever. "But you, Daniel, shut up the words, and seal the book until the time of the end; many shall run to and fro, and knowledge shall increase."

Jesus said the wise ones in our generation, which the Bible calls "the time of the end," are ready with information, called "food" in the passage below, and confidence, which we call faith, to give to others that information they carry at the proper times:

Matthew 24:42-51 *Watch therefore, for you do not know what hour your Lord is coming. But know this, that if the master of the house had known what hour the thief would come, he would have watched and not allowed his house to be broken into. Therefore you also be ready, for the Son of Man is coming at an hour you do not expect. "Who then is a faithful and wise servant, whom his master made ruler over his household, to give them food in due season? Blessed is that servant whom his master, when he comes, will find so doing. Assuredly, I say to you that he will make him ruler over all his goods. But if that evil servant says in his heart, 'My master is delaying his coming,' and begins to beat his fellow servants, and to eat and drink with the drunkards, the master of that servant will come on a day when he is not looking for him and at an hour that he is not aware of, and will cut him in two and appoint him his portion with the hypocrites. There shall be weeping and gnashing of teeth.*

Many will use the excuse "no one knows the day or hour" in order to comfort themselves that there is nothing to be done to prepare for Jesus' return, but that is exactly the OPPOSITE of the point Jesus was making! A carefree attitude towards the return of Jesus is a Satanic deception most of the church in the west has fallen for! Jesus used the analogy of a thief breaking in, and in the analogy, Jesus set Himself up AS THE THIEF! There is great loss waiting for those who refuse to pay attention and participate in Jesus' very specific plans.

Jesus was saying the same thing about greatness in His kingdom that He declared in the Sermon on the Mount: doing and teaching the truths of the hour sets you up for greatness forever... comforting yourself and others to ignore the events of the hour by saying "no one knows for sure" actually is considered REBELLION by Jesus! This careless attitude sets people up to fall away, which means to become offended and quit in the time of intensity! That is what it means to have a portion with hypocrites and to weep and gnash your teeth...that is what it means to be shut out of the kingdom at that exact moment the entire prepared Bride enters in!!

A hypocrite is someone who claims to be one thing, but makes actual choices counter to the identity they claim. According to Jesus and the apostles, there will be many Christians who fall away when the "rubber meets the road" in the seven-year tribulation. They will fall away because of hypocrisy, because they claimed to be ready, but were not actually prepared the way Jesus said to prepare. Because they do not know the plans of their stated savior, nor did they take the time to get ready, they will follow the masses into rebellion against God and actually, out of fear of punishment from earthly powers, give up their salvation. Jesus and the apostles warned over and over about this. Look at what Paul told Timothy about our generation:

2 Timothy 3:1-7 But know this, that in the last days perilous times will come: For men will be lovers of themselves, lovers of money, boasters, proud, blasphemers, disobedient to parents, unthankful, unholy, unloving, unforgiving, slanderers, without self-control, brutal, despisers of good, traitors, headstrong, haughty, lovers of pleasure rather than lovers of God, having a form of godliness but denying its power. And from such people turn away! For of this sort are those who creep into households and make captives of gullible women loaded down with sins, led away by various lusts, always learning and never able to come to the knowledge of the truth.

"Having a form of godliness but denying its power."

Understanding the true power in creation and knowing how to draw on it is the answer to the intensity of Tribulation. This is what is learned by intentionally practicing the Sermon on the Mount.

Paul was not describing lazy people to Timothy! The people that fall away are active. Paul said they are "always learning, yet they never come to the truth!" Paul is describing believers in our day who never enter into the Sermon on the Mount. Instead they listen to the crowds, they hear the messages, they get excited, they dance and sing and tingle, but they never connect these experiences to what Jesus is ACTUALLY doing in their hour of history!

Jesus is preparing the earth, and anyone who will listen, for His return. His return is great. Lots of people will agree with that idea until we start digging into the details, because Jesus' return is also terrible. Most people, in my experience, have no sense of the intense dynamics that they will be here for and need to get ready for.

If a believer refuses to approach their relationship with God from the perspective of what He desires (to be back in the garden He made for His own pleasure), but rather from their own desires (to make the most of their hoped-for 70 or 80 years), they will MISS the very thing their Savior desires to do in their lives! This is what it means to suffer great loss forever.

Jesus comes like a thief! Anyone not ready and paying great attention will suffer great loss! That is what a thief does! This doesn't have to be anyone's fate, though. Anyone who wants to be ready, and wants to value the family story more than their own, can respond now with alertness and vibrancy in agreeing with Jesus' plan. This will cause the humble to avoid loss:

1 Thessalonians 5:1-8 But concerning the times and the seasons, brethren, you have no need that I should write to you. For you yourselves know perfectly that the day of the Lord so comes as a thief in the night. For when they say, "Peace and safety!" then sudden destruction comes upon them, as labor pains upon a pregnant woman. And they shall not escape. But you, brethren, are not in darkness, so that this Day should overtake you as a thief. You are all sons of light and sons of the day. We are not of the night nor of darkness. Therefore let us not sleep, as others do, but let us watch and be sober. For those who sleep, sleep at night, and those who get drunk are drunk at night. But let us who are of the day be sober, putting on the breastplate of faith and love, and as a helmet the hope of salvation.

Right now, everyone who is truly loyal to Jesus will refuse to move on with life UNTIL Jesus returns. This means putting away the pursuits of the "good life" now, and completely investing in the new season Jesus is orchestrating. The Bride has always been expected to live sacrificially, praying sacrificially, fasting and giving sacrificially... training her heart like an athlete. The Bride is supposed to be all about giving away natural strength because she believes in the real and greater power of the supernatural uncreated God.

Man Vs. God

Many false teachers have risen up to connect the Bride to natural strength. Corporate world natural thinking has invaded the Church and she is throwing off the true power found only in sitting before the God of all creation, hearing his instruction, and simply making herself available for Him to use in power. Focusing on the true invisible power behind all of creation by forgoing natural strength is the mode of humility and faith. Instead, many parts of the Church are seeking man-based strategy, when that is the very thing God is in the process of judging! Woe to those who blindly follow the blind.

This earthly logic invading the Church is a Satanic setup to create great offense in the Bride so she will fall away as that very man-based plan falls apart. We don't need advice from the corporate world. The corporate world needs vision and power from our Groom. We don't need to learn how to save more of our money, we need to learn how to give it away extravagantly. We don't need to be more committed to the second amendment, we need to be more committed to the second commandment! There is more power in the name of Jesus than in an entire military brigade, but you must train your heart to live in this reality. That takes time. That must be done in advance.

The Book of Revelation tells the story of the entire Bride globally living in the desert places like the Israelites in the Book of Exodus. The Bride will literally live on manna and water from rocks, multiplying food like Jesus, casting out demons like Jesus, getting resources from fish like Jesus, getting words of knowledge and direction, to the right and to the left, just like her Groom. Jesus said "greater things" will be done by His Bride. We live in the time that word will be true! The Bride will be so much like her groom that the world will know Jesus is the Son of God because of the glory the Bride is releasing. This will require great faith. Faith is confidence, according to Paul:

Hebrews 11:1-2 Faith is the confidence that what we hope for will actually happen; it gives us assurance about things we cannot see. Through their faith, the people in days of old earned a good reputation.

Confidence is learned over time. Those who are faithful with a little confidence...praying for the healing of every sniffle and headache...are given more...eventually restoring sight and limbs. This growing in confidence takes time and focused desire. The oil in the lamp of the 10 Bridesmaids in Matthew 25 is a history of encountering God in times of need. That confidence stored up in the easy times is what lights the lamp of the heart in the dark times. You cannot share your confidence, the actual power of your faith. That confidence is in your heart from your own personal history of encountering God. The Bridesmaid's oil cannot be shared, it MUST be bought at a cost. To purchase the oil, you give up what everyone else is paying attention to, and begin intentionally paying attention to the vast amount of information the Holy Spirit has set in the Bible for you to know. To buy oil you begin restraining your life like a focused Olympian preparing for the biggest race ever, because you humbly realize the Bible says you are going to compete whether you want to or not! This is what Revelation is for: vision for what we are about to enter into! Where there is no vision, there is no focus, and no restraint. That means without Revelation understanding, there is no oil:

Proverbs 29:18 Where there is no revelation, the people cast off restraint; But happy is he who keeps the law.

By the signs of the times, the end time flood of trouble is breaking upon the earth. Right now, the whole Bride is supposed to be working overtime in preparation, looking for those confidence building opportunities, learning to live supernaturally, training their hearts to live in the power of God, which IS the Sermon on the Mount training program. There is a very specific program every person, every family, every church, and every city that wants to can enter in to.

We will go after the vision we have. Right now, many are willing to contend for revival, because the teachers are willing to give vision to the positive aspects of revival, this is exciting and true, but a simple vision for revival WILL NOT CARRY YOU THROUGH THE END TIME TROUBLE. In fact, the limited revival vision will cost many the end time revival because of the promised falling away.

Revival has always come when God's people are desperate for revival! Revival comes when you NEED it.

The end time revival comes in the middle of the greatest trouble the earth has ever seen. You need to endure just to see the HOUR it comes. Did you know God already told us EXACTLY when the final big "R" revival will come?! According to Joel 2:28-32, the end time revival we are contending for will come at the sixth seal, well into the Great Tribulation. Revival comes when we NEED revival to come. You need oil to BE the revival...the light... in the darkness promised to come:

Matthew 25:1-13   "Then the kingdom of heaven shall be likened to ten virgins who took their lamps and went out to meet the bridegroom. Now five of them were wise, and five were foolish. Those who were foolish took their lamps and took no oil with them, but the wise took oil in their vessels with their lamps. But while the bridegroom was delayed, they all slumbered and slept. "And at midnight a cry was heard: 'Behold, the bridegroom is coming; go out to meet him!' Then all those virgins arose and trimmed their lamps. And the foolish said to the wise, 'Give us some of your oil, for our lamps are going out.' But the wise answered, saying, 'No, lest there should not be enough for us and you; but go rather to those who sell, and buy for yourselves.' And while they went to buy, the bridegroom came, and those who were ready went in with him to the wedding; and the door was shut. "Afterward the other virgins came also, saying, 'Lord, Lord, open to us!' But he answered and said, 'Assuredly, I say to you, I do not know you.' "Watch therefore, for you know neither the day nor the hour in which the Son of Man is coming.

Really Clean...For Real

The "falling away" prophesied by Jesus and the disciples is not describing what unbelievers will do, it is describing what will happen in the Church...Jesus' own Body... in the hour of history we live in. You won't hear much about this in the Church right now, because it doesn't preach very well, but it is essential we understand one of the main themes of the end time trouble and the promises that come with it.

God works all things for the good of those who love Him and are called according to His purpose. Even the falling away, one of the worst events in the history of Jesus' Body, will result in the greatest event in Jesus' Bride's history, because the falling away is EXACTLY what will produce a pure and spotless Bride!

Right now, the Bride is pretty wrinkly and spotty, but Jesus is not giving up on the Church! We are not supposed to give up on the Church either. We are supposed to contend for Jesus' Church to be a pure and spotless Bride. She will be, and anyone who AGREES with Jesus' plan to get a pure and spotless Bride will BE a part of that pure and spotless Bride. To agree with the plan, you must know the plan. If you don't understand why Jesus is doing what He is doing, the very plan meant to purify and de-spot the Bride will likely offend you. This is PART OF THE PLAN! Stay with me, and I will explain what I mean.

Jesus has a perfect plan to help the Bride "make herself ready." The plan is most clearly seen in Revelation, although important information about the plan has been sown into the Word from Genesis to Jude. You have to understand the whole counsel of scripture to really grasp what is emerging in the Revelation of Jesus Christ. Revelation is the story of a wedding, and like any good Bride, Jesus' spouse is going to look her most stunning just before the wedding takes place!

The Bride makes herself ready, but Jesus is going to give her the perfect conditions to get ready. Jesus is giving his Bride the dressing room, the curling iron, and the brush, and His true spouse is going to choose to enter into the process and use the tools He has given her! Those who are in the Church for selfish motivations...anything less than to be as much like her Groom as possible...will risk falling away and abandoning their salvation because of offense and fear. This reality is by design. This is a hard word.

The Bride does the readying:

Revelation 19:7-8 Let us be glad and rejoice and give Him glory, for the marriage of the Lamb has come, and His wife has made herself ready." And to her it was granted to be arrayed in fine linen, clean and bright, for the fine linen is the righteous acts of the saints.

But Jesus is also involved by giving the Bride the Spirit and the Word to not just endure the end time events, but to become beautiful through them!

Ephesians 5:25-27 Husbands, love your wives, just as Christ also loved the church and gave Himself for her, that He might sanctify and cleanse her with the washing of water by the word, that He might present her to Himself a glorious church, not having spot or wrinkle or any such thing, but that she should be holy and without blemish.

I am not sure how you do laundry, but at my house, we find the clothes get cleaner by washing them, not fooling ourselves by mixing the dirty with the clean and "declaring" them clean, despite the stains and stink! Just like you would clean up any white clothing, the Bride is going to become pure and spotless not by mixing the dirty with the pure, but by REMOVING the dark spots and the things that make her stink THROUGH AGITATION in the PERFECT CONDITIONS.

When I (I mean Samantha, I am not allowed to operate the dryer anymore) wash my clothes, I put them in the washing machine (end time events perfectly designed to agitate), add some strong soap (the Word of God), some hot water (the Holy Spirit), then I let the machine do its work as the clothes agitate against each other, cleaning themselves by the action of putting them in close proximity in just the right conditions. This is what the Bible calls the "tribulation"...but the process is only half done. Once those clothes are clean, I throw them in the dryer and turn on the heat (Great Tribulation), and the whole load dries out together clean and smelling nice. Then with a lot more heat, I iron my shirts, getting all the wrinkles out. When it is all done, I have some clothes I delight in wearing. This is exactly the process Jesus has selected to get a pure and spotless Bride.

In Luke12 Jesus said "you think peace is going to get the promised Bride? No, not peace, but instead division!" Actually, it is division by agitation. This is intense. You must understand this plan to protect your heart from offense in this hour. Just hearing the plan begins the process of purification, because it forces choices: do I ignore the plan despite the hundreds of verses that support it. Do I oppose those who declare the truth because it makes me uncomfortable? Do I humble myself and start talking to Jesus about this truth, sorting it out for myself?

Jesus is going to let the light agitate the darkness, with the intention of the darkness either agreeing with the light or falling away, just like you would wash your clothes. This is an end time reality:

Luke 12:49-53 "I came to send fire on the earth, and how I wish it were already kindled! But I have a baptism to be baptized with, and how distressed I am till it is accomplished! Do you suppose that I came to give peace on earth? I tell you, not at all, but rather division. For from now on five in one house will be divided: three against two, and two against three. Father will be divided against son and son against father, mother against daughter and daughter against mother, mother-in-law against her daughter-in-law and daughter-in-law against her mother-in-law."

The Bigger Picture

This has ALWAYS been God's plan. God is refining the whole earth to drive evil off the planet. That is what is required for God to come back into His garden. Otherwise, His brightness would destroy the garden. God is mostly interested right now in coming home. Life doesn't happen on planet earth...real life...until God's light is shining here again. Right now we are stuck with the dim light of the sun, but Jesus is preparing the earth to receive a much brighter life source again. Anything dark will be destroyed by his appearing. Anything white will be glorified at His appearing!

Jesus didn't die so we could stay weak and dirty while He is bright and shining. He paid the price that we would have the grace to get bright and shining, too. Bright and shining happens not by laying together in the dirty laundry basket calling ourselves clean by being creepily kind about the stains and stink, but by drawing on the Spirit and the Word to overcome darkness and have victory in the events designed to judge sin and illuminate righteousness!

David understood this reality. The man after God's own heart knew exactly what God was all about 2,000 years before Jesus started the washing machine. Psalm 101, written 3,000 years ago, is all about the falling away in our generation. Look at this Psalm. David was looking way forward anticipating the hours before the arrival of the Groom back on planet earth:

Psalms 101:1-8 I will sing of mercy and justice; To You, O Lord , I will sing praises. I will behave wisely in a perfect way. Oh, when will You come to me? I will walk within my house with a perfect heart. I will set nothing wicked before my eyes; I hate the work of those who fall away; It shall not cling to me. A perverse heart shall depart from me; I will not know wickedness. Whoever secretly slanders his neighbor, Him I will destroy; The one who has a haughty look and a proud heart, Him I will not endure. My eyes shall be on the faithful of the land, That they may dwell with me; He who walks in a perfect way, He shall serve me. He who works deceit shall not dwell within my house; He who tells lies shall not continue in my presence. Early I will destroy all the wicked of the land, That I may cut off all the evildoers from the city of the Lord .

I am going to paraphrase this profound Psalm by David in my own words to convey what I see here:

I am watching what I do, how I live, and what I rejoice in, because I am longing for your return, God. I am especially careful in my own house...Your house...God. I don't let the wicked stuff go unchecked there, God, because I am committed to my heart being pure and the hearts of those you love being safe. I watch what the people around me are doing...especially the ones who claim to know you and love you like I do. I am seriously going to fight against wickedness by being careful who I run with. I am not going to wink, smile, and overlook wickedness in my house...Your house...God. For the slanderers, I am going to destroy their place by exposing them. As for the proud and haughty, I am not going to pretend we are friends. Instead, I am going to look for people faithful to truth. Those are the ones I will let come close to me in friendship and in service. Those trying to completely follow you...they are the ones I am going to partner with, not those who pretend to love you but are clearly only doing what makes them more comfortable, or look more important or good. I am going to destroy the influence of the liars and cut them off before they grow too tall, by speaking the truth to them.

This is intense, but this is exactly what Jesus is releasing into His Church in this hour all over the globe. It has always been God's plan that this reality, which started in Jerusalem 2,000 years ago, would mature in our day. The first coming of Jesus, which marked the "conception" of the Day of the Lord, was when Jesus sowed this truth into the earth. The second coming of Jesus will mark the "delivery" of the Day of the Lord, when the fruit that came from what Jesus first sowed will be harvested. The harvest process and the birth process are the two main analogies in the Bible to describe the events that span from Acts 2 until our generation. Numerous times the Bible describes the process God has selected to renew all things as being like the birth of a baby:

Romans 8:22-23 For we know that the whole creation groans and labors with birth pangs together until now. Not only that, but we also who have the firstfruits of the Spirit, even we ourselves groan within ourselves, eagerly waiting for the adoption, the redemption of our body.

John 16:20-22 Most assuredly, I say to you that you will weep and lament, but the world will rejoice; and you will be sorrowful, but your sorrow will be turned into joy. A woman, when she is in labor, has sorrow because her hour has come; but as soon as she has given birth to the child, she no longer remembers the anguish, for joy that a human being has been born into the world. Therefore you now have sorrow; but I will see you again and your heart will rejoice, and your joy no one will take from you.

Birth of a Harvest

Right now, truth is emerging, just like a baby is born. The truth was planted like a seed in Jerusalem nearly 2,000 years ago, and it has been growing in the earth all this time. Right now the fruit of truth, called a pure and spotless Bride, is about to be delivered. Delivery is intense. What happens in the secret place of the tummy for 9 months gets all wild, crazy, exciting, frightful, painful, and joyful all in the span of a few weeks culminating in the worst and best moment ever. This is what Jesus described His coming like. This is really simple. You don't need to be a theologian to get this. Moms and dads who have watched birth go down are way more qualified to understand the end times than the greatest Bible scholar who is unwilling to humble himself and just take the main and plain meaning of the Bible.

Truth is light, and light is being delivered...growing stronger and stronger...louder and louder...as it's full emergence draws near. Light is OFFENSIVE to darkness, and I hate to be the bearer of bad news, but Jesus' Bride-to-be still has a lot of dark spots. Though light is what was planted by Jesus when He commissioned His Bride to go enforce His victory from Jerusalem outward to the ends of the earth, the enemy has planted darkness among the light.

Both the light and the dark has been maturing for 2,000 years. We got some real good stuff in the field and some real bad stuff in the field, and it is all growing in CLOSE proximity. This is what the parable of the wheat and the tares is all about.

It is important to understand the specific nature of the end time parables. Much can be learned from the simple analogies Jesus used. The parable of the wheat and tares contains a ton of information about why the falling away must happen!

*Matthew 13:24-30, 36-43 Another parable He put forth to them,
saying: "The kingdom of heaven is like a man who sowed good seed in
his field; but while men slept, his enemy came and sowed tares among
the wheat and went his way. But when the grain had sprouted and
produced a crop, then the tares also appeared. So the servants of the
owner came and said to him, 'Sir, did you not sow good seed in your
field? How then does it have tares?' He said to them, 'An enemy has
done this.' The servants said to him, 'Do you want us then to go and
gather them up?' But he said, 'No, lest while you gather up the tares
you also uproot the wheat with them. Let both grow together until
the harvest, and at the time of harvest I will say to the reapers, "First
gather together the tares and bind them in bundles to burn them, but
gather the wheat into my barn." ...*

*... " Then Jesus sent the multitude away and went into the house. And
His disciples came to Him, saying, "Explain to us the parable of the
tares of the field." He answered and said to them: "He who sows the
good seed is the Son of Man. The field is the world, the good seeds are
the sons of the kingdom, but the tares are the sons of the wicked one.
The enemy who sowed them is the devil, the harvest is the end of the
age, and the reapers are the angels. Therefore as the tares are
gathered and burned in the fire, so it will be at the end of this age.
The Son of Man will send out His angels, and they will gather out of His
kingdom all things that offend, and those who practice lawlessness,
and will cast them into the furnace of fire. There will be wailing and
gnashing of teeth. Then the righteous will shine forth as the sun in the
kingdom of their Father. He who has ears to hear, let him hear!*

The Harvesters are Harvested

This is a parable about the Church. The whole parable is about
the close proximity of the sons of the evil one to the sons of the
kingdom...so close their roots are right there mingling together. They
are feeding on the same food! This is MOSTLY a parable about people
that go to Church together. Many misunderstand this parable to extend
back to Adam and Eve and make it an encouragement to believers and a
warning to unbelievers. This is not the emphasis of this passage.

The Bible is not generally a warning to the world. The Bible is
mostly a warning to believers. Unbelievers do not believe in God, or

believe the Bible is true. We are the warning to unbelievers. Jesus says this parable starts with the Son of Man sowing the good seed, or the believers following Him. Jesus was sowing the seed even as He told this parable.

Jesus lays out the scenario perfectly. God give us eyes to see! The field is the world, where we live. The harvest is the end of the age, the hour WE live in. The angels are the reapers. They are not plucking people by their hair off the earth. We must understand the nature of the partnership between angels and mankind as God's government in the earth.

The angels are the ones assigned to the nations and over the resources of the earth. Good and bad angels are "wrestling" based on the intercession, or expressed desire, of the people, and the events that are culminating with that wrestling are producing the reaping. The governing of the earth from heaven has always worked this way, and it is driving the whole earth to the last days. Just like birth, this process intensifies, and more interaction between mankind and angles will be the result. This will reap the harvest!

Look at what Daniel learned of this partnership between man and angles, and the wrestling that resulted in end time truth emerging:

Daniel 10:12-14 Then he said to me, "Do not fear, Daniel, for from the first day that you set your heart to understand, and to humble yourself before your God, your words were heard; and I have come because of your words. But the prince of the kingdom of Persia withstood me twenty-one days; and behold, Michael, one of the chief princes, came to help me, for I had been left alone there with the kings of Persia. Now I have come to make you understand what will happen to your people in the latter days, for the vision refers to many days yet to come."

The end time events are entirely driven by mankind interceding, or expressing desire, and partnering with angels, and that is what "swings the sickle" of reaping:

Revelation 7:2-3 Then I saw another angel ascending from the east, having the seal of the living God. And he cried with a loud voice to the four angels to whom it was granted to harm the earth and the sea, saying, "Do not harm the earth, the sea, or the trees till we have sealed the servants of our God on their foreheads."

Revelation 8:3-5 Then another angel, having a golden censer, came and stood at the altar. He was given much incense, that he should offer it with the prayers of all the saints upon the golden altar which was before the throne. And the smoke of the incense, with the prayers of the saints, ascended before God from the angel's hand. Then the angel took the censer, filled it with fire from the altar, and threw it to the earth. And there were noises, thunderings, lightnings, and an earthquake.

This concept of mankind offering prayers of intercession that move angels day and night is the primary focus, or reality, of the pure and spotless Bride becoming pure and spotless. God is orchestrating trouble in the earth, and those who agree with Him know His plan and start doing their part, which is interceding in wholehearted love for God as their primary activity, which spills over into going out from the places of intercession and being the answers to their own prayers, as angels partner with the intercessors and open doors for us to love neighbors as we love ourselves.

Mark 12:28-34 Then one of the scribes came, and having heard them reasoning together, perceiving that He had answered them well, asked Him, "Which is the first commandment of all?" Jesus answered him, "The first of all the commandments is: 'HEAR, O ISRAEL, THE LORD OUR GOD, THE LORD IS ONE. AND YOU SHALL LOVE THE LORD YOUR GOD WITH ALL YOUR HEART, WITH ALL YOUR SOUL, WITH ALL YOUR MIND, AND WITH ALL YOUR STRENGTH.' This is the first commandment. And the second, like it, is this: 'YOU SHALL LOVE YOUR NEIGHBOR AS YOURSELF.' There is no other commandment greater than these." So the scribe said to Him, "Well said, Teacher. You have spoken the truth, for there is one God, and there is no other but He. And to love Him with all the heart, with all the understanding, with all the soul, and with all the strength, and to love one's neighbor as oneself, is more than all the whole burnt offerings and sacrifices." Now when Jesus saw that he answered wisely, He said to him, "You are not far from the kingdom of God." But after that no one dared question Him.

These are the two greatest commandments that will draw everyone who wants it nearer and nearer to the kingdom, and it actually starts with gathering together in unity and praying and singing together. This is exactly what David hired 24,000 people to get started in his day, called the Tabernacle of David, which released the greatest prophetic explosion of light in the darkness, as recorded in the Psalms, the earth had seen to that point. THIS is what Jesus is rebuilding all over the globe for our day as a safe place...a barn, so to speak... as the intensity of the events increase:

Amos 9:9-12 "For surely I will command, And will sift the house of Israel among all nations, As grain is sifted in a sieve; Yet not the smallest grain shall fall to the ground. All the sinners of My people shall die by the sword, Who say, 'The calamity shall not overtake nor confront us.' "On that day I will raise up The tabernacle of David, which has fallen down, And repair its damages; I will raise up its ruins, And rebuild it as in the days of old; That they may possess the remnant of Edom, And all the Gentiles who are called by My name," Says the LORD who does this thing.

Shaking and Sifting
God has told His people that His plan is a harvest plan...to "shake everything that can be shaken." This refers to the threshing process in the time of harvest. The threshers take the grain and the stuff that gets caught up with it, then they throw the whole lot into the air and let the wind separate the good wheat from the junk, which has less weight to it. A wind of trouble, orchestrated by God, has already started blowing in a noticeable way. More intensity is coming.

This trouble, called tribulation, meant to refine the harvest, is offensive to those in the Body of Christ who do not understand the plan. Jesus said in the Olivet Discourse (Matthew 24, Mark 13, Luke 21) that this reality would create the conditions of the falling away. Now is the time to find out the answer and declare the truth within the house...like David said in Psalm 101...so that as many as possible will be steady through the harvest season and gathered into the barns.

Many oppose this message because it offends them. They are mostly more worried about what other people might think than they are worried about absolutely understanding what the Bible says about Jesus plans and humbly agreeing with them. They have their own plans for greatness they don't want anything to interrupt. God isn't interested in the plans of men. His plans are perfect. Our lesser plans steal our own future if left unchecked. God calls our plans rebellion if they don't match His.

The revelation of truth will expose the motivations and the strengths of everyone first in the house of God, and then later outside the house of God. How can God be just in judging the nations if His own house cannot stand in the same light? That is why tribulation starts in His house.

1 Peter 4:17-19 For the time has come for judgment to begin at the house of God; and if it begins with us first, what will be the end of those who do not obey the gospel of God? Now "IF THE RIGHTEOUS ONE IS SCARCELY SAVED, WHERE WILL THE UNGODLY AND THE SINNER APPEAR?" Therefore let those who suffer according to the will of God commit their souls to Him in doing good, as to a faithful Creator.

Speaking of the final years leading to the return of the Messiah, the Lord said that His people would fall into great error specifically because spiritual leaders were more interested in earthly pleasures than in learning and teaching the very intense thing the Lord was doing in their day. There is a blessing in the Book of Revelation for reading and teaching the book, because it is hard to commit to. The end time message is offensive to many because it forces a decision. You cannot love God, understand Revelation, and remain neutral.

In Isaiah 28, God delivers a stark message to the priests and prophets of His people. God starts out describing the way those loyal to Jesus will see Him as a "crown of glory" and a "diadem of beauty", God then relates this to the willingness of those who love his just, but intense, plans, which require "turning back the battle at the gate" of Jerusalem. This is referring to those who oppose, primarily through intercessional warfare, the plans of the antichrist. A battle IS necessary. Few want to hear about the coming battle, but everyone needs to. For those who refuse to enter in and understand God's end time plan, there will be great trouble.

Listen to this intense end-time passage from Isaiah:

Isaiah 28:5-13 In that day the LORD of hosts will be For a crown of glory and a diadem of beauty To the remnant of His people, For a spirit of justice to him who sits in judgment, And for strength to those who turn back the battle at the gate. But they also have erred through wine, And through intoxicating drink are out of the way; The priest and the prophet have erred through intoxicating drink, They are swallowed up by wine, They are out of the way through intoxicating drink; They err in vision, they stumble in judgment. For all tables are full of vomit and filth; No place is clean. "Whom will he teach knowledge? And whom will he make to understand the message? Those just weaned from milk? Those just drawn from the breasts? For precept must be upon precept, precept upon precept, Line upon line, line upon line, Here a little, there a little." For with stammering lips and another tongue He will speak to this people, To whom He said, "This is the rest with which You may cause the weary to rest," And, "This is the refreshing"; Yet they would not hear. But the word of the LORD was to them, "Precept upon precept, precept upon precept, Line upon line, line upon line, Here a little, there a little," That they might go and fall backward, and be broken And snared and caught.

Because God's plan is very specific, and requires an understanding of the full council of scripture, it takes time and attention to understand, comprehend, and learn the plan. It requires an intentional study of the Bible and a growing conversation with the Holy Spirit.

"What are you doing in THIS hour Lord?" is the question that should be on our lips in this generation continually, for all of creation has longed for the days WE live in. What a tragedy to get to see this hour and miss the very thing God is doing! That is why Jesus warned His disciples, those that knew Him, over and over that His return would come like a thief in the night for many!

Matthew 24:37-39 But as the days of Noah were, so also will the coming of the Son of Man be. For as in the days before the flood, they were eating and drinking, marrying and giving in marriage, until the day that Noah entered the ark, and did not know until the flood came and took them all away, so also will the coming of the Son of Man be.

Why Does No One Know?

Think about that analogy for a minute. Many use the warning Jesus gave to be ready as an excuse to NOT get ready. Jesus didn't say "no one knows the day or hour" so people would do nothing. He said it so they wouldn't wait to get ready. If a big flood is coming, and, if Jesus expects you to build an ark, you better get hammering. God knows human nature is to procrastinate on the hard stuff, so Jesus said: I am not going to tell you when, get ready now! The entire western Church has taken what those first disciples understood correctly as a warning and turned it into an excuse for distraction. All of those first disciples were ready for the trouble that is coming:

1 John 2:18 Little children, it is the last hour; and as you have heard that the Antichrist is coming, even now many antichrists have come, by which we know that it is the last hour.

What the Holy Spirit is saying to the Bride is MUCH different than those who hold themselves up as leaders in Jesus' body...pastors and prophets alike... are mostly saying to the Bride in this hour. I am not saying this to be mean, I am saying it because the Bible has warned about this for THOUSANDS of years. Do not listen to what I, or anyone else, tells you about this hour. You must abide in Jesus yourself. Use the warnings people like me are giving to prod you to search the Word. Don't use the false comfort many are giving as an excuse to do nothing.

The intense warning to believers is intended by God. That is why God does not correct anyone for giving the warnings in the wrong season. However, not once, but over and over He says those who allow the people to fall into false comfort will be responsible for many sorrows:

Jeremiah 28:11-13 And Hananiah spoke in the presence of all the people, saying, "Thus says the LORD: 'Even so I will break the yoke of Nebuchadnezzar king of Babylon from the neck of all nations within the space of two full years.' " And the prophet Jeremiah went his way. Now the word of the LORD came to Jeremiah, after Hananiah the prophet had broken the yoke from the neck of the prophet Jeremiah, saying, "Go and tell Hananiah, saying, 'Thus says the LORD: "You have broken the yokes of wood, but you have made in their place yokes of iron."

Many pastors and prophets, with the intention of comforting and encouraging, are ACTUALLY putting iron yokes on the very ones they are sent to warn and protect. Listen to the encouragement, but you must find out what the Bible says for yourself and begin the conversation with God. If you don't abide in Jesus, you WILL miss what God is doing. Relying on other people to tell you what God is saying is not acceptable to Jesus. It is great to receive from others, but only as an aide to your own conversation with the Lord. Otherwise, you won't bear fruit. Listen to what Jesus told His disciples shortly before He went to the cross:

John 15:1-8 "I am the true vine, and My Father is the vinedresser. Every branch in Me that does not bear fruit He takes away; and every branch that bears fruit He prunes, that it may bear more fruit. You are already clean because of the word which I have spoken to you. Abide in Me, and I in you. As the branch cannot bear fruit of itself, unless it abides in the vine, neither can you, unless you abide in Me. "I am the vine, you are the branches. He who abides in Me, and I in him, bears much fruit; for without Me you can do nothing. If anyone does not abide in Me, he is cast out as a branch and is withered; and they gather them and throw them into the fire, and they are burned. If you abide in Me, and My words abide in you, you will ask what you desire, and it shall be done for you. By this My Father is glorified, that you bear much fruit; so you will be My disciples.

Unity With Jesus vs. Unity For Jesus
I am not speaking against unity. Unity in the Body is very important, but there are many kinds of unity. Unity based on agreeing with other people about Jesus is "man-based" unity. This is unacceptable to the Lord.

The unity God wants is based on us agreeing with God about other people, not agreeing with other people about God.

Jesus-centered unity is the only unity that will endure. Man-based unity will lead many astray. That is what Psalm 14 is all about. It takes God to love God, and it takes God to love other people. That is why the first commandment is love GOD with all your heart, soul, mind, and strength, and the second is to love others as you love yourself. Only by having your OWN deep and ongoing abiding conversation with God can you bear the fruit of love and please God. This is a massive part of God's end time plan. If you cannot hear God in this hour, that should be the primary issue you are addressing. You need to hear God more and more as the day of His return nears.

This concept is becoming more and more important as the days wear on. This is why: the Bible is clear that many IN the Church will fall away from the truth. According to the Bible, the falling away is primarily based on the lack of information regarding God's end time plan. In the passage from Isaiah 28 that I quoted, God tells Isaiah the "falling into error" was related to their unwillingness to be taught "line by line, precept upon precept." Let's look at that passage again:

Isaiah 28:9-10 "Whom will he teach knowledge? And whom will he make to understand the message? Those just weaned from milk? Those just drawn from the breasts? For precept must be upon precept, precept upon precept, Line upon line, line upon line, Here a little, there a little."

Labor of Love

Here God is releasing an important insight: it takes TIME and ATTENTION to actually understand this amazing end time plan. Simply thinking in the old patterns of understanding will not cut it. The priests and prophets in this passage are simply running on old information that they are unwilling to add to because they were more interested in the worldly pleasure. So God says the most amazing thing: if you won't learn in humility from those I raise up to teach you, you will have to learn the hard way...from foreigners who don't even speak your language as they overrun you in terror:

Isaiah 28:11-13 For with stammering lips and another tongue He will speak to this people, To whom He said, "This is the rest with which You may cause the weary to rest," And, "This is the refreshing"; Yet they would not hear. But the word of the LORD was to them, "Precept upon precept, precept upon precept, Line upon line, line upon line, Here a little, there a little," That they might go and fall backward, and be broken And snared and caught.

The Bible is clear that there is much trouble coming. The trouble is entirely designed to lead the willing into Jesus' leadership. Understanding the judgments in this light, and learning to love them, is essential. Jesus' leadership will never wane. If you do not learn to love His judgments precept by precept, you will learn them the hard way. This is really simple, but who will listen? It requires faith to enter into the warnings and promises of the Bible before they are obvious to the entire world. Jesus is looking for those that will take the time to figure out...to learn...what He is doing in this hour. Listen to what Jesus told His disciples about His return:

Luke 18:7-8 And shall God not avenge His own elect who cry out day and night to Him, though He bears long with them? I tell you that He will avenge them speedily. Nevertheless, when the Son of Man comes, will He really find faith on the earth?"

Did you hear that? Jesus told His disciples that He would return to His own elect (that is believers) who "cry out day and night to Him, though He bears long with them" (that means it is going to take some time of crying out and figuring out what HE is waiting for). What are Jesus' friends in the final days crying out for?...VENGEANCE. That means that great trouble is coming. This is super clear in the Bible. The return of Jesus is like a baby being born. That glorious process of birth comes with great intensity and trial. There is no other birth process. This requires advanced understanding and preparation.

Not caring enough to learn what is happening in the months and years leading up to the return of Jesus is a great offense to God. Many died to get this truth to you! If you live in the generation all of creation has longed to see, you have a great obligation to sort out what it is you are supposed to do with this great gift. If you don't, the gift becomes a great curse.

Not only does not understanding Jesus' specific plans leave you and your family vulnerable to becoming offended and quitting in absolute loyalty to Jesus, it also leaves you and your family vulnerable to BETRAYING other believers. This is why: soon, fundamental Christianity will be illegal globally. This is because the antichrist is going to attempt a global government from His home country, which I believe for reasons to deep to delve into here, is the USA. That means anyone declaring that the world's greatest leader is actually the world's greatest deceiver will be considered to a traitor globally, but most vehemently in the USA. Listen to what Jesus said EVERY disciple can expect, globally, in the years leading up to His appearing:

Matthew 24:9-14 "Then they will deliver you up to tribulation and kill you, and you will be hated by all nations for My name's sake. And then many will be offended, will betray one another, and will hate one another. Then many false prophets will rise up and deceive many. And because lawlessness will abound, the love of many will grow cold. But he who endures to the end shall be saved. And this gospel of the kingdom will be preached in all the world as a witness to all the nations, and then the end will come.

The True Jesus Will Divide
True Christianity...I mean intensely loyal-to-Jesus-as-the-only-savior-who-is-coming-to-defeat-the-man-of-lawlessness-Christianity ...will certainly be illegal in every country. There are already numerous news articles about how our local and state governments are armed to the hilt, and fundamental Christianity is documented to be considered a possible source of right-wing terrorism by the Department of Homeland Security. There is a perfect storm of police state trouble brewing in America, and globally. The Church is SUPPOSED to address this.

However, according to Jesus, there will be a watered-down Christianity that will compromise with the antichrist governments of the earth. You can already see great schisms appearing in the Church over the most important and controversial issues: Israel, eschatology, the truth and inerrancy of God's Word, and the truth about sin. The division primarily falls along the line of "what does the Bible say is true?" vs. "what does society WANT to be true?" Political correctness is literally pulling the Church in half. Many are more afraid of what people might think about any given issue than what GOD thinks about any given issue! Siding with people over God, or fearing the fallout from offending people rather than fearing the fallout from offending God, is the great error at the heart of the great falling away. This must happen BEFORE Jesus returns:

2 Thessalonians 2:2-3 *not to be soon shaken in mind or troubled, either by spirit or by word or by letter, as if from us, as though the day of Christ had come. Let no one deceive you by any means; for that Day will not come unless the falling away comes first, and the man of sin is revealed, the son of perdition,*

This is really bad news for the Church, because it means that many, for fear of the personal cost of staying true to Jesus, will actually side with the government AGAINST other Christians, all in the name of Jesus! This has happened numerous times in the past.

For example, the Nazi's hijacked compromising elements in the protestant German church in order to carry out the horrors of the holocaust. There was a movement called the "German Christian" or "Duetsche Christen" movement who's betrayal of both Christians and Jews is well documented. Listen to this excerpt from the Wikipedia page for the German Christian movement:

" The Deutsche Christen were supportive of the Nazi ideas about race. They issued public statements that Christians in Germany with Jewish ancestors "remain Christians in a New Testament sense, but are not German Christians." Also they supported the call from the Nazi party platform for a "positive Christianity" that does not stress human sinfulness. Some went so far as to call for removal of the "Jewish" Old Testament from the Bible. Their symbol was a traditional Christian cross with a swastika in the middle and the group's German initials "D" and "C". It was claimed and remembered, as a "fact", that the Jews had killed Christ, thus appealing to and actively encouraging existing anti-Semitic sentiment among Christians in Germany."

Consider what is currently happening in the American Church. In the news over the last couple of years as some of the largest American denominations are casting off the Biblical teaching about Israel. Sin has become the thing many denominations not only have blurred the line on, but now actively espouse an anti-Biblical stance on. Even fundamental mainline denominations have little to no insight on the evil nature of America's involvement in peace and security negotiations for Israel while simultaneously empowering those sworn to Israel's destruction (i.e., Iran and the Muslim Brotherhood). Because they refuse to come back to the books of Daniel and Revelation for insight into the events of our day...symbolizing, minimizing, and symbolically fulfilling the Great Tribulation that is bearing down on the whole globe....they teach their people error. They put iron yokes where there was only an easy yoke, if the people would humble themselves and respond to the Biblical warnings. A hard lesson is coming.

The result of this casual attitude towards the truth of the Word colliding with the intensity of Jesus' end time plan is promised to result in massive division in Jesus' body. Listen to what Jesus prophesied for the Bride:

Mark 13:12-14 Now brother will betray brother to death, and a father his child; and children will rise up against parents and cause them to be put to death. And you will be hated by all for My name's sake. But he who endures to the end shall be saved. "So when you see the 'ABOMINATION OF DESOLATION,' spoken of by Daniel the prophet, standing where it ought not" (let the reader understand), "then let those who are in Judea flee to the mountains.

It isn't those who warn that cause the betrayal, it is those that ignore the massive amount of information about what is coming because they refuse to take the time, humble themselves, learn, and begin teaching what Jesus taught...all of it. Jesus, in this chronological passage from Matthew 24, described the nature of betrayal that will touch the Church BEFORE the Great Tribulation, which begins with the erection of a statue in the Holy Place in Jerusalem, called the abomination of desolation.

The Cost of Not Responding
If we don't begin teaching the truth about the intense events to come, preparing each other to stand in the hour of intensity, when it comes like a flood, many will fall in line with the government to save their own skin. Praying and teaching NOW, will prevent MUCH trouble later, but many are unwilling to take the time to learn about what the Bible is clear about coming in the final generation.

I don't know of one church leader who doesn't say "we are living in the last days," but I know of almost none that are willing to actually search out the true nature of the last days, let alone teach it. This is great error. Don't take anyone's word for what is coming, but for heaven's sake find out for yourself the particular dynamics the Bible describes. We all need each other to understand the pitfalls of falling away and the effect it has on communities. The stakes are VERY high.

In this next passage from Ezekiel 13, the Lord describes to Ezekiel the consequences of the false prophets prophesying "peace and safety" when great trouble is coming. Pay attention to the context of this passage. First in verses 1 through 16, God addresses the false prophets in Jerusalem, and the great trouble that comes on Israel because they are unprepared. But then, God addresses the Bride, or the "daughters of Ezekiel's people." God says the offspring of Israel has its own false prophets. False prophets prophesy out of the hopes in their own hearts, and will actually cause the rebellion which results in "veiled" murderers hunting true Christians. This has happened before, and is promised to happen globally in the end time, which this passage clearly is describing:

Ezekiel 13:17-23 "Likewise, son of man, set your face against the daughters of your people, who prophesy out of their own heart; prophesy against them, and say, 'Thus says the Lord GOD: "Woe to the women who sew magic charms on their sleeves and make veils for the heads of people of every height to hunt souls! Will you hunt the souls of My people, and keep yourselves alive? And will you profane Me among My people for handfuls of barley and for pieces of bread, killing people who should not die, and keeping people alive who should not live, by your lying to My people who listen to lies?" 'Therefore thus says the Lord GOD: "Behold, I am against your magic charms by which you hunt souls there like birds. I will tear them from your arms, and let the souls go, the souls you hunt like birds. I will also tear off your veils and deliver My people out of your hand, and they shall no longer be as prey in your hand. Then you shall know that I am the LORD. "Because with lies you have made the heart of the righteous sad, whom I have not made sad; and you have strengthened the hands of the wicked, so that he does not turn from his wicked way to save his life. Therefore you shall no longer envision futility nor practice divination; for I will deliver My people out of your hand, and you shall know that I am the LORD." ' "

The Lord says through the prophet "And will you profane Me among My people for handfuls of barley and for pieces of bread," this is a direct reference to the motivating factor (a need for food) driving the false prophets as their lies are judged in third seal in Revelation 6:

Revelation 6:5-6 When He opened the third seal, I heard the third living creature say, "Come and see." So I looked, and behold, a black horse, and he who sat on it had a pair of scales in his hand. And I heard a voice in the midst of the four living creatures saying, "A quart of wheat for a denarius, and three quarts of barley for a denarius; and do not harm the oil and the wine."

Famine is coming as the world system breaks down. God's people who respond to the warnings and get ready in faith will live on supernatural provision. But, many of God's people whom the storm takes by surprise, out of fear of famine touching their own families, will fall in line with the government just to stay alive. Those who fall away will help the governments of the earth track down those faithful to the true message of Jesus.

We need to hear the warning. Great division is coming to the Church, just as it did in Nazi Germany.

The way to protect your community is to teach the truth. We can all flourish in faith together when we realize trouble is coming, and there is much we can do now to get ready, primarily by building Sermon on the Mount living in our town, which will be answered with supernatural power and provision. Understanding the end time events gives vision to the people to actually press in to the Sermon on the Mount and a supernatural lifestyle.

Picture the Christians who are persecuted in the Middle East right now. Have you seen the pictures of Islamic radicals that hunt Christians in Egypt, Libya, Nigeria, Syria, and Iraq? Have you seen how they wear hoods? Do you hear the Ezekiel warning? Hooded executioners that think they are serving God are going global, according to the Bible. Do you see ANYTHING in the news that disagrees with this? Are you watching? Do you know what to watch for?

Loosing the Bonds of Loyalty Increases Bondage to Darkness

There is a movement to integrate faiths that is gaining much traction in this hour. In 2014, the Pope traveled to Israel with an Islamic Imam and a Rabbi, which resulted in an interfaith prayer meeting at the Vatican. Mainline denominations in America are boycotting Israel and siding with Islamic Palestinians in the great Middle East conflict. The Bible tells us CLEARLY what this is leading to. Do you understand it? Are you ready? This is the hour that information regarding the end time events will make all the difference in how people prepare, but what is happening to those that sound the alarms? Do you hear them and respond, or are they just an interesting curiosity, like John the Baptist was to many in his day? Now is the hour to get ready, but many just like hearing about getting ready. That is not enough.

Ezekiel 33:30-33 "As for you, son of man, the children of your people are talking about you beside the walls and in the doors of the houses; and they speak to one another, everyone saying to his brother, 'Please come and hear what the word is that comes from the LORD.' So they come to you as people do, they sit before you as My people, and they hear your words, but they do not do them; for with their mouth they show much love, but their hearts pursue their own gain. Indeed you are to them as a very lovely song of one who has a pleasant voice and can play well on an instrument; for they hear your words, but they do not do them. And when this comes to pass—surely it will come—then they will know that a prophet has been among them."

The Glorious Answer to the Falling Away

YOU CAN GET READY TO NOT JUST ENDURE THE TRIBULATION, BUT TO FLOURISH IN THE TRIBULATION, but you must face the truth of the tribulation head-on to get ready. This requires humility. This is the Bride's greatest hour, but only a pure and spotless Bride will glory in what is about to transpire. Many who don't have a vision for changing in response to the hour will fall away, according to Jesus in Revelation 2 and 3, and Revelation 19. Pure and spotless is for real...there will be no other kind of Bride:

Revelation 19:7-8 Let us be glad and rejoice, and let us give honor to Him. For the time has come for the wedding feast of the Lamb, and His bride has prepared herself. She has been given the finest of pure white linen to wear." For the fine linen represents the good deeds of God's holy people.

Step 1: Admit There is a Problem

The falling away is a PROMISED problem for the Bride. Paul said it MUST happen first. The first step to fixing a problem is ADMITTING there could be one. Many refuse to see the problem of the falling away, because, in arrogance, they do not believe THEY could fall away. Many pastors ignore the falling away, because they either don't understand it, or realize that to correct people to get them ready would mean they would have to admit they missed the mark on some of their teaching in the past. Dealing rightly with the consequences of the falling away requires humility.

A simple Bible search with your phone or computer for the phrase "fall away" will reveal several Biblical warnings given to the beloved of God to guard against falling away. Either God doesn't know what to teach, or there is a REAL risk to believers of falling away. Mark my words, if you do not humble yourself and listen to the words of warning in the Bible, you are a prime candidate to fall away. If you do not get ready in advance, you will be susceptible to running down the same road that Peter went down when Jesus warned him of his un-readiness. Look at this exchange between Peter and Jesus:

Luke 22:31-36 And the Lord said, "Simon, Simon! Indeed, Satan has asked for you, that he may sift you as wheat. But I have prayed for you, that your faith should not fail; and when you have returned to Me, strengthen your brethren." But he said to Him, "Lord, I am ready to go with You, both to prison and to death." Then He said, "I tell you, Peter, the rooster shall not crow this day before you will deny three times that you know Me." And He said to them, "When I sent you without money bag, knapsack, and sandals, did you lack anything?" So they said, "Nothing." Then He said to them, "But now, he who has a money bag, let him take it, and likewise a knapsack; and he who has no sword, let him sell his garment and buy one.

This exchange reveals much more than we could go into right now, but I want to highlight the broad theme: Peter thought he was ready for what was next because he considered himself ready to fight and die. Jesus said Peter did not understand his own heart and that he was NOT ready. Then Jesus told all the disciples to GET READY in agreement with JESUS' plan.

You don't need to be ready to die for what comes next. You don't need to be ready to get raptured. You need to be ready to endure and do the great commission. When Jesus told His disciples to get ready that night, He was talking to them parabolically. He was saying they needed the Sermon on the Mount...true wealth...true provision....and an understanding of the Word, which is the sword and worth more than their very clothes. You might think: "Tom, how do you know this is what Jesus was saying?!" Let's look at what happens next:

Matthew 26:50-53 But Jesus said to him, "Friend, why have you come?" Then they came and laid hands on Jesus and took Him. And suddenly, one of those who were with Jesus stretched out his hand and drew his sword, struck the servant of the high priest, and cut off his ear. But Jesus said to him, "Put your sword in its place, for all who take the sword will perish by the sword. Or do you think that I cannot now pray to My Father, and He will provide Me with more than twelve legions of angels?

Step 2: Believe in the Gospel...For Real

We know that the main line of preparation Jesus wanted the disciples to use was to pray. In the Garden of Gethsemane, Jesus pleaded with the disciples to pray three times, yet they were too tired and distracted for that. They were relying on a false sense of preparation...they thought swords would do it! They had swords with them that night according to Luke 22:49! According to John 18:10 it was PETER who cut off the ear of the servant of the high priest. Peter WAS ready to make a split second decision, if FORCED, to fight with human strength for Jesus. BUT, Peter was NOT ready to endure what Jesus had planned. Unwilling to humble himself and find out why Jesus told him he was unready, Peter had to suffer the consequences of His error. Three times that night when simply asked if he was with Jesus, Peter denied it. Peter was completely unready, yet had no idea, because the Spirit is willing, but the flesh is weak. This is EXACTLY what Jesus told Peter in the garden hours before the fruit of Peter's decision to ignore the warning would be tested:

Matthew 26:40-41 Then He came to the disciples and found them sleeping, and said to Peter, "What! Could you not watch with Me one hour? Watch and pray, lest you enter into temptation. The spirit indeed is willing, but the flesh is weak."

If Jesus allowed one of His best friends to go through this, what kind of arrogance keeps us from believing we should prepare for at least as much? The stakes are higher in the generation of the falling away. We have been given much more than Peter had that night. We have the New Testament, we have the Holy Spirit indwelling us, and we live in the generation that is seeing all the signs. To fall away NOW has much greater consequences than Peter suffered. Because of the Spirit who indwells believers after the resurrection of Jesus, falling away is now permanent, according to Paul:

Hebrews 6:4-6 For it is impossible for those who were once enlightened, and have tasted the heavenly gift, and have become partakers of the Holy Spirit, and have tasted the good word of God and the powers of the age to come, if they fall away, to renew them again to repentance, since they crucify again for themselves the Son of God, and put Him to an open shame.

Step 3: Teach the Real Gospel...All of It
We must prepare to endure. It is a lie that says "no one knows the day or hour" as an excuse to delay readiness, and the unfortunate error of a pre-tribulation rapture theology, started in 1830, that lulls the very ones called to be ready by praying like their very lives depended on it, to instead slumber. Watch and pray, for you can clearly see the hour...you see it, right?

Peter was restored and we can learn a lot from it. When Jesus restored Peter, how did he do it? Did Jesus say "Peter, now are you REALLY ready to die for me?" No! Jesus said the oddest thing, unless you understand the falling away. Jesus said this:

John 21:17 He said to him the third time, "Simon, son of Jonah, do you love Me?" Peter was grieved because He said to him the third time, "Do you love Me?" And he said to Him, "Lord, You know all things; You know that I love You." Jesus said to him, "Feed My sheep.

Jesus restored Peter by teaching him what "being ready" really means. Actually, Jesus had already taught Peter this same basic truth at least twice before. Jesus said "feed my sheep." What does this mean? It is really simple. To be ready means two things, First: to love God with all your heart, mind, soul, and strength; and the second is like it: to love your neighbor as yourself. Before you say "I already do that" realize that this is the theological truth behind the practical end time reality. Do you want to hear how Jesus phrased the practical end time application of the two greatest commandments? Here it is:

Matthew 24:44-51 Therefore you also be ready, for the Son of Man is coming at an hour you do not expect. "Who then is a faithful and wise servant, whom his master made ruler over his household, to give them food in due season? Blessed is that servant whom his master, when he comes, will find so doing. Assuredly, I say to you that he will make him ruler over all his goods. But if that evil servant says in his heart, 'My master is delaying his coming,' and begins to beat his fellow servants, and to eat and drink with the drunkards, the master of that servant will come on a day when he is not looking for him and at an hour that he is not aware of, and will cut him in two and appoint him his portion with the hypocrites. There shall be weeping and gnashing of teeth.

Being ready means ready to teach others the end time plan and make choices yourself that agree with it. Being foolish means not paying attention to the end time plan because "no one could know the day or hour." We need to be all about feeding others because we are lovesick for Jesus. The food is the Word of God. Understanding and teaching the end time plans of Jesus is what it means to "feed others." That is why Revelation contains this promise:

Revelation 1:3 Blessed is he who reads and those who hear the words of this prophecy, and keep those things which are written in it; for the time is near.

To "read and keep" the Revelation prophecy means that you know the plan and read it to the Church, and you make decision that agree with it. It means to "do and teach". Doing and teaching the stuff that agrees with Revelation is to do and teach the Sermon on the

Mount! The Sermon on the Mount is the glorious answer to the riddle of Revelation. Being a wise servant is the answer to the question "who can stand" in Revelation 6:17!

Revelation 6:15-17 *And the kings of the earth, the great men, the rich men, the commanders, the mighty men, every slave and every free man, hid themselves in the caves and in the rocks of the mountains, and said to the mountains and rocks, "Fall on us and hide us from the face of Him who sits on the throne and from the wrath of the Lamb! For the great day of His wrath has come, and who is able to stand?"*

We are to Teach What Jesus Taught

Jesus taught the end time plans to the Church. If you study Revelation for any length of time, you find out that the Book of Revelation is the story of the wedding between Jesus and His Bride. Like any wedding, there is a cast of people that are involved (Revelation 1 through 4), there are plans that must be made and started (Revelation 5), a preparing of the wedding location by getting rid of anything that doesn't agree with the wedding and decorating it with things that agree with the wedding (Revelation 6 through 16), relatives that will get upset (Revelation 17 and 18), and finally a glorious beautiful Bride who looks her best ever just before the Groom and Bride are joined together (Revelation 19) and they go out to make their home and life together (Revelation 20 through 22).

In Revelation 2 and 3, Jesus applied these three steps of readiness to the Bride-to-be, who seriously risks falling away. She is a bit wrinkled, dirty, and divided, but She is HIS. Jesus is committed to helping her get ready, but for love, He refuses to make her get ready. If she doesn't want to get ready, she cannot get married. Jesus is too grand to be forever joined to an unequally-yoked Bride. He has all the power to get us ready, but only those who wholeheartedly love Him more than their own lives will enter in and begin getting ready. Not ready to die, but to "feed His Sheep," which means making their entire lives about gathering in the harvest within, AND outside of, the Church.

Many within the Church need to be readied with Jesus' end time plan, and many outside of the Church need both salvation AND the end time plan. This will all occur in the season of the greatest trouble the earth has ever seen, just as Daniel was told:

Daniel 12:1-3 "At that time Michael shall stand up, The great prince who stands watch over the sons of your people; And there shall be a time of trouble, Such as never was since there was a nation, Even to that time. And at that time your people shall be delivered, Every one who is found written in the book. And many of those who sleep in the dust of the earth shall awake, Some to everlasting life, Some to shame and everlasting contempt. Those who are wise shall shine Like the brightness of the firmament, And those who turn many to righteousness Like the stars forever and ever.

"Wise shall shine"...Remember what Jesus said about the wise and faithful end time servant in Matthew 24? They lead many to RIGHTEOUSNESS. That happens through doing and teaching the Sermon on the Mount (Matthew 5, 6, and 7). Similar to the promise of blessing in Revelation 1:3, we find another promise of greatness or loss in Matthew 5:19, right after Jesus tells the crowd the roadmap for growing holiness, called the Beatitudes. Listen to the promise for learning and doing the Beatitudes:

Matthew 5:18-19 For assuredly, I say to you, till heaven and earth pass away, one jot or one tittle will by no means pass from the law till all is fulfilled. Whoever therefore breaks one of the least of these commandments, and teaches men so, shall be called least in the kingdom of heaven; but whoever does and teaches them, he shall be called great in the kingdom of heaven.

In Revelation 2 and 3, Jesus looks at His spouse in our day, and then picks out 7 Churches way back in John's day that represent the main identities of the Church in our day...I call these the "Seven Characteristic Churches" of Revelation. Five of the seven churches: Ephesus, Pergamos, Thyatira, Sardis, and Laodicea are so out of agreement with Jesus that they risk falling away unless they change. He says this to them directly. Look at the warnings Jesus gives these Churches:

Ephesus
Revelation 2:4-5 Nevertheless I have this against you, that you have left your first love. Remember therefore from where you have fallen;

repent and do the first works, or else I will come to you quickly and remove your lampstand from its place—unless you repent.

Thyatira
Revelation 2:20-25 Nevertheless I have a few things against you, because you allow that woman Jezebel, who calls herself a prophetess, to teach and seduce My servants to commit sexual immorality and eat things sacrificed to idols. And I gave her time to repent of her sexual immorality, and she did not repent. Indeed I will cast her into a sickbed, and those who commit adultery with her into great tribulation, unless they repent of their deeds. I will kill her children with death, and all the churches shall know that I am He who searches the minds and hearts. And I will give to each one of you according to your works. "Now to you I say, and to the rest in Thyatira, as many as do not have this doctrine, who have not known the depths of Satan, as they say, I will put on you no other burden. But hold fast what you have till I come.

Sardis
Revelation 3:1-3 "And to the angel of the church in Sardis write, 'These things says He who has the seven Spirits of God and the seven stars: "I know your works, that you have a name that you are alive, but you are dead. Be watchful, and strengthen the things which remain, that are ready to die, for I have not found your works perfect before God. Remember therefore how you have received and heard; hold fast and repent. Therefore if you will not watch, I will come upon you as a thief, and you will not know what hour I will come upon you.

Laodicea
Revelation 3:15-20 "I know your works, that you are neither cold nor hot. I could wish you were cold or hot. So then, because you are lukewarm, and neither cold nor hot, I will vomit you out of My mouth. Because you say, 'I am rich, have become wealthy, and have need of nothing'—and do not know that you are wretched, miserable, poor, blind, and naked— I counsel you to buy from Me gold refined in the fire, that you may be rich; and white garments, that you may be clothed, that the shame of your nakedness may not be revealed; and anoint your eyes with eye salve, that you may see. As many as I love, I

*rebuke and chasten. Therefore be zealous and repent. Behold, I stand
at the door and knock. If anyone hears My voice and opens the door, I
will come in to him and dine with him, and he with Me.*

Listen friends: According to Revelation 2 and 3, five-
sevenths…seventy one percent… of the Church in the end times is out of
agreement with Jesus and risks falling away unless she repents and
changes her way of living! If she repents, Jesus will help her
"overcome." Overcome what, Tom?! Overcome the tribulation, which
begins in Revelation 5. This is intended to be simple to see.

Now, there are two churches Jesus does not correct: the first is
Smyrna, which is the church currently being murdered or threatened
with murder for their belief in Jesus. They are enduring the persecution
in advance that will soon envelope the whole globe. Smyrna is not
corrected. If you go to a church like Smyrna (already under intense
persecution) and are prepared to endure persecution and threats of
death for the next decade, or so, pay no mind to the warning of falling
away…you probably "got this." I imagine that describes NO ONE, or at
least very few, reading this book.

Philadelphia, the second church that does not get corrected is
Philadelphia. This is the night and day praying church. Wait a second,
Tom, how can you make such a bizarre claim?! It is easy, Jesus Himself
says it. Look at how Jesus addresses the church at Philadelphia:

*Revelation 3:7-13 "And to the angel of the church in Philadelphia
write, 'These things says He who is holy, He who is true, "HE WHO HAS
THE KEY OF DAVID, HE WHO OPENS AND NO ONE SHUTS, AND SHUTS
AND NO ONE OPENS": "I know your works. See, I have set before you
an open door, and no one can shut it; for you have a little strength,
have kept My word, and have not denied My name. Indeed I will make
those of the synagogue of Satan, who say they are Jews and are not,
but lie—indeed I will make them come and worship before your feet,
and to know that I have loved you. Because you have kept My
command to persevere, I also will keep you from the hour of trial
which shall come upon the whole world, to test those who dwell on the
earth. Behold, I am coming quickly! Hold fast what you have, that no
one may take your crown. He who overcomes, I will make him a pillar
in the temple of My God, and he shall go out no more. I will write on
him the name of My God and the name of the city of My God, the New*

Jerusalem, which comes down out of heaven from My God. And I will write on him My new name. "He who has an ear, let him hear what the Spirit says to the churches." '

David's Key

The Philadelphia Church has "keyed in" to the Key of David that opens the door Jesus was talking about. David started a night and day prayer center in Jerusalem called the Tabernacle, as an expression of his wholehearted love for God. Night and day seeking of God overflowed into a love for those around him (brotherly love, or Philadelphia). Being a "pillar in the temple of God"...one who never goes out...was the "One thing" David desired, as expressed so clearly in Psalm 27:4. Solomon turned David's tabernacle worship movement into the temple worship movement when he built a permanent building for the night and day prayer. David was so committed to this reality that he hired 24,000 people to keep day and night worship going in Jerusalem. 4,000 of those people were just musicians. David said he did all of this because of His great affection for the House of God. David wanted God back on earth where God belongs. He was unwilling to enjoy the good life until God was back home:

1 Chronicles 29:1-3 Furthermore King David said to all the assembly: "My son Solomon, whom alone God has chosen, is young and inexperienced; and the work is great, because the temple is not for man but for the LORD God. Now for the house of my God I have prepared with all my might: gold for things to be made of gold, silver for things of silver, bronze for things of bronze, iron for things of iron, wood for things of wood, onyx stones, stones to be set, glistening stones of various colors, all kinds of precious stones, and marble slabs in abundance. Moreover, because I have set my affection on the house of my God, I have given to the house of my God, over and above all that I have prepared for the holy house, my own special treasure of gold and silver...

David did all of this because being in the presence of God was his one desire. But, David also knew something else. Making God your only desire is what gives you all the power to overcome every enemy. Jesus said in the Sermon on the Mount "Seek God's kingdom first, and all the rest will be added unto you." Do you know what you will need in the end time trouble? Everything the antichrist will try to take away from you: money, food, relationships, and physical might, to name a few. Do you know how to get that in a way that no one can take from you? Seek God first with all your mind soul and strength! Then God will put you on a rock that cannot move while everything else is shaking. Listen to David in Psalm 27:

Psalms 27:3-6 Though an army may encamp against me, My heart shall not fear; Though war may rise against me, In this I will be confident. One thing I have desired of the LORD, That will I seek: That I may dwell in the house of the LORD All the days of my life, To behold the beauty of the LORD, And to inquire in His temple. For in the time of trouble He shall hide me in His pavilion; In the secret place of His tabernacle He shall hide me; He shall set me high upon a rock. And now my head shall be lifted up above my enemies all around me; Therefore I will offer sacrifices of joy in His tabernacle; I will sing, yes, I will sing praises to the LORD.

Desiring One Thing
This IS Jesus' end time plan for His Bride in the broadest strokes. There is so much more to know, but this is where you start: in the place of building 24 hour prayer, or "David's Tabernacle." If you have 24 hour prayer in your town, ask God to show you how to get involved. If you don't, pray that it starts. Caring about the Biblical answer and making it your answer is all that is required to get started. This is wisdom. Listen to what the prophet Amos said about our generation:

Amos 9:8-12 "I, the Sovereign LORD, am watching this sinful nation of Israel. I will destroy it from the face of the earth. But I will never completely destroy the family of Israel, " says the LORD. "For I will give the command and will shake Israel along with the other nations as grain is shaken in a sieve, yet not one true kernel will be lost. But all the sinners will die by the sword—all those who say, 'Nothing bad will happen to us.' "In that day I will restore the fallen house of David. I will repair its damaged walls. From the ruins I will rebuild it and restore its former glory. And Israel will possess what is left of Edom and all the nations I have called to be Mine. " The LORD has spoken, and He will do these things.

24-Hour Desire for Holiness

Learning to build 24-hour prayer with a bunch of other Christians from all over your city is the "incubator" for the seven divided Churches to become one pure and spotless Bride by the end of the trouble. 24-hour prayer and worship REQUIRES a commitment to the Sermon on the Mount. Building night and day prayer takes time in prayer, money, fasting, humility, and an awareness of spiritual poverty. It requires forgiving offenses, it requires dying to your own agenda, it requires being spitefully used and still smiling and saying "I am doing this for Jesus, so it is ok!"

If you will endure dealing with people who love Jesus, in tight confines, being lame to you, then you will be made ready to overcome the Great Tribulation when it is people who HATE Jesus that want to persecute you. The Great Tribulation is barreling at you like a freight train, whether you like it or not. David's Tabernacle is the barn that the true grains will come into through the shaking. Get in the barn now, and STAY in the barn despite all the people who are troublesome in the barn, and you will be safe from the storm. The Biblical solution to becoming a holy family kept safe through the process designed entirely to sift out a family is so simple anyone can do it, but so simple few will. Who are you going to choose to be?

Jesus said "if you live by the sword, you will die by the sword." Growing in holiness by learning to desire it with others 24-hours a day is the only Biblical plan for the end time Church. If your plan to endure is any different than agreeing with Jesus' plans, you are living in arrogance. Don't take my word for what Jesus' plans are, but for heaven's sake, and the sake of your own family and friends, find out for yourself what His plans are and agree with them. Now is the time!

Luke 18:7-8 Even he rendered a just decision in the end. So don't you think God will surely give justice to His chosen people who cry out to Him day and night? Will He keep putting them off? I tell you, He will grant justice to them quickly! But when the Son of Man returns, how many will He find on the earth who have faith?"

The Throne of David - 3

The falling away is the single-greatest threat to the end time church in this hour. The falling away happens because the Church moves further and further from truth of Jesus' leadership and closer and closer to the false promises of the antichrist's leadership. The anecdote for falling away is to love the truth:

2 Thessalonians 2:9-11 The coming of the lawless one is according to the working of Satan, with all power, signs, and lying wonders, and with all unrighteous deception among those who perish, because they did not receive the love of the truth, that they might be saved. And for this reason God will send them strong delusion, that they should believe the lie,

The truth of Jesus' government is the truth we are supposed to love. The truth that Jesus IS, in fact, no matter what the world may say, the "only one worthy" to lead the people of the earth forever:

Isaiah 9:6-7 For unto us a Child is born, Unto us a Son is given; And the government will be upon His shoulder. And His name will be called Wonderful, Counselor, Mighty God, Everlasting Father, Prince of Peace. Of the increase of His government and peace There will be no end, Upon the throne of David and over His kingdom, To order it and establish it with judgment and justice From that time forward, even forever. The zeal of the Lord of hosts will perform this.

Jesus will sit on David's throne. <u>God</u> is going to sit on a <u>man's</u> throne!! This should be a stunning statement to every man, woman, and child! If I want to understand what it is Jesus came to begin, and will return to complete, I need to understand David, and how he ruled from Israel.

The Heart of God

Understanding David is incredibly important to understanding the generation we live in, because we live in the generation of the "pure and spotless Bride." A Bride is after the heart of her groom. If David is the man after God's heart, then the Bride is going to have to look, sound, think, and act a LOT like David.

Acts 13:21-22 And afterward they asked for a king; so God gave them Saul the son of Kish, a man of the tribe of Benjamin, for forty years. And when He had removed him, He raised up for them David as king, to whom also He gave testimony and said, 'I HAVE FOUND DAVID THE SON OF JESSE, A MAN AFTER MY OWN HEART, WHO WILL DO ALL MY WILL.'

God called David a man after God's own heart. One facet of this truth is that if I want to understand God's heart, I can look to David and see great revelation of what truly matters to God. David's life demonstrates that it isn't strength or experience that God values, but rather humility.

Matthew 18:3-4 ..."Assuredly, I say to you, unless you are converted and become as little children, you will by no means enter the kingdom of heaven. Therefore whoever humbles himself as this little child is the greatest in the kingdom of heaven.

Humility isn't pretending to have a lower value than you do. God does not value dishonesty. Humility is seeing clearly, and then being honest about, what I bring to the table and what God brings. If I am totally honest, I will see that all I bring to the table is my "yes"...my desire....and that God brings everything else...all the strength, experience, and provision.

This was the difference between Saul and David. Saul valued his own strength, experience, and provision above God's. Saul was a towering and strong man. He came from a powerful family. Saul had all the natural strength and wealth that was required for people to follow him:

1 Samuel 9:1-2 There was a wealthy, influential man named Kish from the tribe of Benjamin. He was the son of Abiel, son of Zeror, son of Becorath, son of Aphiah, of the tribe of Benjamin. His son Saul was the most handsome man in Israel—head and shoulders taller than anyone else in the land.

Everyone thought Saul was the kind of guy to lead Israel in strength, but God was not impressed. When Jesus came, Israel missed His true strength because once again they were looking for a Saul. Even in this hour, the Bible promises one last "Saul" will offer his services to Israel to make peace. God rejected Saul because of his unwillingness to choose to live humbly in partnership with God:

I Samuel 16:1 Now the Lord said to Samuel, "How long will you mourn for Saul, seeing I have rejected him from reigning over Israel? Fill your horn with oil, and go; I am sending you to Jesse the Bethlehemite. For I have provided Myself a king among his sons."

Humility Allows God's Strength to Flow Through
David did not operate in the spirit of Saul, who trusted in his own strength and resources to do something impressive for God in the sight of other people. Instead, David trusted God and used what God had provided in order to get closer to God. Nearness to God was David's primary motivation.   David chose this "one thing" focus of living because God had shown Himself strong on David's behalf time and time again. David had a history of building faith in God. The more David trusted God, the more God revealed Himself to David until David knew that he could not be defeated as long as he was living in God's leadership:

1 Samuel 17:33-40 "Don't be ridiculous!" Saul replied. "There's no way you can fight this Philistine and possibly win! You're only a boy, and he's been a man of war since his youth." But David persisted. "I have been taking care of my father's sheep and goats," he said. "When a lion or a bear comes to steal a lamb from the flock, I go after it with a club and rescue the lamb from its mouth. If the animal turns on me, I catch it by the jaw and club it to death. I have done this to both lions and bears, and I'll do it to this pagan Philistine, too, for he has defied the armies of the living God! The LORD who rescued me from the claws of the lion and the bear will rescue me from this Philistine!" Saul finally consented. "All right, go ahead," he said. "And may the LORD be with you!" Then Saul gave David his own armor—a bronze helmet and a coat of mail. David put it on, strapped the sword over it, and took a step or two to see what it was like, for he had never worn such things before. "I can't go in these," he protested to Saul. "I'm not used to them." So David took them off again. He picked up five smooth stones from a stream and put them into his shepherd's bag. Then, armed only with his shepherd's staff and sling, he started across the valley to fight the Philistine.

David grew in his reliance on God to be His strength. This was David's theology:

Psalms 37:3-7 Trust in the Lord , and do good; Dwell in the land, and feed on His faithfulness. Delight yourself also in the Lord , And He shall give you the desires of your heart. Commit your way to the Lord , Trust also in Him, And He shall bring it to pass. He shall bring forth your righteousness as the light, And your justice as the noonday. Rest in the Lord , and wait patiently for Him; Do not fret because of him who prospers in his way, Because of the man who brings wicked schemes to pass.

David's theology was based on this principal: God wants to be my strength and my leader. My job is to give God more and more agreement with this truth...to die to the desires that drive everyone else around me and voluntarily to turn my desire to Him...to know Him more, so I can agree with His leadership more. It takes God to love God, and David knew loving God was the place of greatest strength. Jesus agreed:

Matthew 6:31-33 "So don't worry about these things, saying, 'What will we eat? What will we drink? What will we wear?' These things dominate the thoughts of unbelievers, but your heavenly Father already knows all your needs. Seek the Kingdom of God above all else, and live righteously, and He will give you everything you need.

God doesn't view leadership the way mankind does. Mankind typically views leadership from a top down perspective, trading power for loyalty. This is how Satan leads. The trading of power for loyalty is a clear indicator that Satan is involved. Trading power for loyalty is what began Satan's rebellion, as he promised the angels a better position in his rebellious kingdom than the position they had under God's perfect leadership. Listen to the charge against Lucifer:

Ezekiel 28:15-16 You were perfect in your ways from the day you were created, Till iniquity was found in you. "By the abundance of your trading You became filled with violence within, And you sinned; Therefore I cast you as a profane thing Out of the mountain of God; And I destroyed you, O covering cherub, From the midst of the fiery stones.

Many, even in the Church, trade power for loyalty as their main way of relating to others. This is not the nature of God. God is a father. His kingdom is a family. To seek His kingdom first is to grow in your knowledge of Him as a Father...a leader, a provider, a loving protector...as the top priority in life. This naturally results in a good family that gives to others freely, since God is unlimited in provision, time, and opportunity, and loves His entire family. Tapping into His heart grows this reality in our lives. This is what God has always desired: to be face to face with mankind, partnering with man in forever increasing God's government over all of creation. A father partnering with His sons and daughters in the family business forever:

John 17:24 "Father, I desire that they also whom You gave Me may be with Me where I am, that they may behold My glory which You have given Me; for You loved Me before the foundation of the world.

God living physically face to face with mankind in partnership with the goal of increasing the government of God over creation is what God called "very good" in Genesis 1:

Genesis 1:27-31 So God created man in His own image; in the image of God He created him; male and female He created them. Then God blessed them, and God said to them, "Be fruitful and multiply; fill the earth and subdue it; have dominion over the fish of the sea, over the

*birds of the air, and over every living thing that moves on the earth."
And God said, "See, I have given you every herb that yields seed which
is on the face of all the earth, and every tree whose fruit yields seed; to
you it shall be for food. Also, to every beast of the earth, to every bird
of the air, and to everything that creeps on the earth, in which there is
life, I have given every green herb for food"; and it was so. Then God
saw everything that He had made, and indeed it was very good. So the
evening and the morning were the sixth day.*

God NEVER changes:

*James 1:17 Whatever is good and perfect comes down to us from God
our Father, who created all the lights in the heavens. He never changes
or casts a shifting shadow.*

What God wants from His children is not complicated. Want to
know God's will for your life? It is easy: for you to make your main
priority...what you spend your time, money, emotion, and desire
on...hearing God and obeying Him more so that He can fulfill every
dream He knit into your heart. Many are aware of the dreams for
greatness the Father knit into their heart, but in pride and rebellion,
they attempt to fulfill those dreams apart from the leadership of the
Father who authored them. This is the foolishness of a faithless Saul.
To understand the faith of David, we MUST understand the
rebellion...the witchcraft...of Saul. Trying to operate in God's power
apart from God's leadership is the Biblical definition of witchcraft. This
aspect of Saul's story is essential to grasp:

*I Samuel 15:1-23 Samuel also said to Saul, "The Lord sent me to anoint
you king over His people, over Israel. Now therefore, heed the voice of
the words of the Lord . Thus says the Lord of hosts: 'I will punish
Amalek for what he did to Israel, how he ambushed him on the way
when he came up from Egypt. Now go and attack Amalek, and utterly
destroy all that they have, and do not spare them. But kill both man
and woman, infant and nursing child, ox and sheep, camel and
donkey.' "*

So Saul gathered the people together and numbered them in Telaim, two hundred thousand foot soldiers and ten thousand men of Judah. And Saul came to a city of Amalek, and lay in wait in the valley. Then Saul said to the Kenites, "Go, depart, get down from among the Amalekites, lest I destroy you with them. For you showed kindness to all the children of Israel when they came up out of Egypt." So the Kenites departed from among the Amalekites. And Saul attacked the Amalekites, from Havilah all the way to Shur, which is east of Egypt. He also took Agag king of the Amalekites alive, and utterly destroyed all the people with the edge of the sword. But Saul and the people spared Agag and the best of the sheep, the oxen, the fatlings, the lambs, and all that was good, and were unwilling to utterly destroy them. But everything despised and worthless, that they utterly destroyed.

Now the word of the Lord came to Samuel, saying, "I greatly regret that I have set up Saul as king, for he has turned back from following Me, and has not performed My commandments." And it grieved Samuel, and he cried out to the Lord all night. So when Samuel rose early in the morning to meet Saul, it was told Samuel, saying, "Saul went to Carmel, and indeed, he set up a monument for himself; and he has gone on around, passed by, and gone down to Gilgal."

Then Samuel went to Saul, and Saul said to him, "Blessed are you of the Lord ! I have performed the commandment of the Lord ." But Samuel said, "What then is this bleating of the sheep in my ears, and the lowing of the oxen which I hear?" And Saul said, "They have brought them from the Amalekites; for the people spared the best of the sheep and the oxen, to sacrifice to the Lord your God; and the rest we have utterly destroyed."

Then Samuel said to Saul, "Be quiet! And I will tell you what the Lord said to me last night." And he said to him, "Speak on." So Samuel said, "When you were little in your own eyes, were you not head of the tribes of Israel? And did not the Lord anoint you king over Israel? Now the Lord sent you on a mission, and said, 'Go, and utterly destroy the sinners, the Amalekites, and fight against them until they are consumed.' Why then did you not obey the voice of the Lord ? Why did you swoop down on the spoil, and do evil in the sight of the Lord ?"

And Saul said to Samuel, "But I have obeyed the voice of the Lord , and gone on the mission on which the Lord sent me, and brought back Agag king of Amalek; I have utterly destroyed the Amalekites. But the people took of the plunder, sheep and oxen, the best of the things which should have been utterly destroyed, to sacrifice to the Lord your God in Gilgal."

So Samuel said: "Has the Lord as great delight in burnt offerings and sacrifices, As in obeying the voice of the Lord ? Behold, to obey is better than sacrifice, And to heed than the fat of rams. For rebellion is as the sin of witchcraft, And stubbornness is as iniquity and idolatry. Because you have rejected the word of the Lord , He also has rejected you from being king."

This was the rejected theology of Saul: that God didn't mind Saul doing things his own way, as long as Saul tried to accomplish what God wanted done. This rationalization of disobedience is great error, because it places the man above God. What God desires is humility demonstrated by obedience.   David humbled himself and obeyed the Lord because David loved God more than anything else. Jesus said this:

John 14:15 "If you love Me, keep My commandments.

We MUST get correct understanding of this simple verse. The common misunderstanding of God lines up with Saul's theology: if I love God I should prove it by my obedience. David would wholeheartedly disagree. David would say "If I love God, I can't help but obey Him." David believed obedience flowed naturally from a lovesick heart. Saul valued strength and self focus over love.

God is not trying to hide His desire from us. His desire is plain to see, and because God is truth, everything He has ever said will ALWAYS be true. God's definition of "Very Good" will never change. The Bible is the story of the process God has chosen to bring everything mankind degraded back to "very good." David understood the process and desired, more than anything else, to agree with it:

Psalms 27:4-5 One thing I have desired of the Lord , That will I seek: That I may dwell in the house of the Lord All the days of my life, To behold the beauty of the Lord , And to inquire in His temple. For in the time of trouble He shall hide me in His pavilion; In the secret place of His tabernacle He shall hide me; He shall set me high upon a rock.

This desire perfectly lined up with God's desire. David said "God, I want to be with you where YOU are more than anything. This is where I am safe. God responded "David, that is what I desire more than anything, too!"

David understood the implications of His desire. Many will claim to want to love God more than anything, but they refuse to "count the cost."

Luke 14:26-33 (NLT) "If you want to be My disciple, you must hate everyone else by comparison—your father and mother, wife and children, brothers and sisters—yes, even your own life. Otherwise, you cannot be My disciple. And if you do not carry your own cross and follow Me, you cannot be My disciple. "But don't begin until you count the cost. For who would begin construction of a building without first calculating the cost to see if there is enough money to finish it? Otherwise, you might complete only the foundation before running out of money, and then everyone would laugh at you. They would say, 'There's the person who started that building and couldn't afford to finish it!' "Or what king would go to war against another king without first sitting down with his counselors to discuss whether his army of 10,000 could defeat the 20,000 soldiers marching against him? And if he can't, he will send a delegation to discuss terms of peace while the enemy is still far away. So you cannot become My disciple without giving up everything you own.

David understood that to get close to God, you must agree with God about who is leading. God will never come to occupy second place, because that would violate the truth of who He is. You cannot have God's presence without His leadership. You might be able to impact the earth through faith, or cast out demons by the authority of God for a while…you might be able to hear knowledge and wisdom that astounds other men from the other side of the veil …but you CANNOT have the presence and agreement of God…the smile of God…on your life without humility.

We are in the hour that many in the Church will be operating in great demonstrations of power, healing the sick, casting out demons, and prophesying, all in the name of Jesus. But, Jesus said many would actually be operating in rebellion, which the Bible calls witchcraft. According to Jesus, those in rebellion won't know it!...they will be surprised when they meet Jesus face to face and He judges not their gifting or their works...but their motivation. Many operate in the name of Jesus to build their own ministry. They want to build something for God rather than use all their strength to humble themselves like children and get to know more and more, the heart of the Father:

Matthew 7:15-27 "Beware of false prophets, who come to you in sheep's clothing, but inwardly they are ravenous wolves. You will know them by their fruits. Do men gather grapes from thornbushes or figs from thistles? Even so, every good tree bears good fruit, but a bad tree bears bad fruit. A good tree cannot bear bad fruit, nor can a bad tree bear good fruit. Every tree that does not bear good fruit is cut down and thrown into the fire. Therefore by their fruits you will know them. "Not everyone who says to Me, 'Lord, Lord,' shall enter the kingdom of heaven, but he who does the will of My Father in heaven. Many will say to Me in that day, 'Lord, Lord, have we not prophesied in Your name, cast out demons in Your name, and done many wonders in Your name?' And then I will declare to them, 'I never knew you; depart from Me, you who practice lawlessness!' "Therefore whoever hears these sayings of Mine, and does them, I will liken him to a wise man who built his house on the rock: and the rain descended, the floods came, and the winds blew and beat on that house; and it did not fall, for it was founded on the rock. "But everyone who hears these sayings of Mine, and does not do them, will be like a foolish man who built his house on the sand: and the rain descended, the floods came, and the winds blew and beat on that house; and it fell. And great was its fall."

A Growing Storm
Look at the news, and scan the horizon. A storm is coming. Jesus warned us about what the conditions of the storm will look like. At the same time a storm is growing, many are seeking "revival" as their main goal. In this hour many are growing in their knowledge and skill in using the name of Jesus to heal the sick, cast out demons and prophesy,

but seeking revival is not the Biblical mandate. The mandate is to seek, above all other things, to submit to God's leadership even when it offends the mind of man.

Revival is great, and revival IS coming in a measure the earth has never seen. Everyone loyal to Jesus, all flesh, will have the Spirit poured out on them in signs and wonders in a manifestation greater than the Acts 2 Church. But, signs and wonders, and leading many to the Church, will also be done by those in the Church actually ignoring, if not opposing, the leadership of God. They won't state that, because like Saul, they will believe they are serving God.

In this hour we need hearts like David and hearts like Jesus. Jesus did not value operating in great power, but rather valued complete allegiance to the Father. Jesus operated in great power as He drew on the leadership of the Father. Jesus is the firstborn of many sons and daughters.

Philippians 2:5-9 Let this mind be in you which was also in Christ Jesus, who, being in the form of God, did not consider it robbery to be equal with God, but made Himself of no reputation, taking the form of a bondservant, and coming in the likeness of men. And being found in appearance as a man, He humbled Himself and became obedient to the point of death, even the death of the cross. Therefore God also has highly exalted Him and given Him the name which is above every name,

John 5:19 Then Jesus answered and said to them, "Most assuredly, I say to you, the Son can do nothing of Himself, but what He sees the Father do; for whatever He does, the Son also does in like manner.

The Bible promises that many who operate in signs and wonders will reject this simple principle of submission. They will fear the opinions of their peers more than they fear the penetrating gaze of God that judges not the works, but the intention behind the works. For a season those operating in rebellion may get away with it and look holy to the people, but only truth will pass through the fire of tribulation. Now is the time to begin understanding exactly what will pass through the fire of the next several years, because the smoke is already on the horizon:

1 Corinthians 3:11-14 For no other foundation can anyone lay than that which is laid, which is Jesus Christ. Now if anyone builds on this foundation with gold, silver, precious stones, wood, hay, straw, each one's work will become clear; for the Day will declare it, because it will be revealed by fire; and the fire will test each one's work, of what sort it is. If anyone's work which he has built on it endures, he will receive a reward.

King David's Enduring Legacy

David was a king like no other. The Bible says David was fierce in both war AND worship. This is the strangest combination! On earth, we may see a great king who is confident in battle because he is confident in himself or the strength of his army, but a "worshiping warrior" is a strange thing! The worshiping warrior's confidence in battle comes from the place of humility! Listen to David's war strategy, which he declared on the day he finally became king:

II Samuel 22:1-4 Then David spoke to the Lord the words of this song, on the day when the Lord had delivered him from the hand of all his enemies, and from the hand of Saul. And he said: "The Lord is my rock and my fortress and my deliverer; The God of my strength, in whom I will trust; My shield and the horn of my salvation, My stronghold and my refuge; My Savior, You save me from violence. I will call upon the Lord , who is worthy to be praised; So shall I be saved from my enemies.

David established his throne with this strategy in mind. This is the throne JESUS will sit upon. We must understand David's throne if we want to understand Jesus' plans to remake the earth!

Luke 1:31-32 And behold, you will conceive in your womb and bring forth a Son, and shall call His name JESUS. He will be great, and will be called the Son of the Highest; and the Lord God will give Him the throne of His father David.

David did not adopt the mindset of the pagan kings, or his predecessor, Saul, by attempting to consolidate his power in paying favors to the strong and making compromising alliances once he came to power. No! In fact, David did the opposite! Rather than get more confident in himself by aligning with those as strong or stronger, than he was, David became more infatuated with, and more confident in God, the One TRULY stronger than himself. David grew in his desire to serve God as his main priority.

David was not corrupted by the power given to him because David kept his gaze on a greater power. Not only did he fear that greater power, David fell in love with the greatest power in all of creation! Knowing the One with all the power was David's one desire:

Psalms 27:1-5 The Lord is my light and my salvation; Whom shall I fear? The Lord is the strength of my life; Of whom shall I be afraid? When the wicked came against me To eat up my flesh, My enemies and foes, They stumbled and fell. Though an army may encamp against me, My heart shall not fear; Though war may rise against me, In this I will be confident. One thing I have desired of the Lord , That will I seek: That I may dwell in the house of the Lord All the days of my life, To behold the beauty of the Lord , And to inquire in His temple. For in the time of trouble He shall hide me in His pavilion; In the secret place of His tabernacle He shall hide me; He shall set me high upon a rock.

David, unlike any king before him, sought God first, and all the rest was added unto him. This is the "Key of David" (remember that phrase, it will be super important to you) that unlocked heaven in Israel during David's reign. Jesus confirmed this is a good strategy for life:

Matthew 6:33 But seek first the kingdom of God and His righteousness, and all these things shall be added to you.

Christians tend to make "seeking God first" a "theological ideal" that they will someday "get to", but David made this his practical governmental strategy with the Tabernacle of David! According to the Bible, the entire Bride is going to have to agree with David about this practical strategy by the time Jesus returns! The time is short, friends. It is with THIS key, David's Key, that the Bride will respond to God and unlock the heavens. Day and night prayer to music will literally open heaven on earth and usher in the King of Glory!

By the time the global Bride is done seeking God first and letting the rest be added unto her, there will be an open heaven on earth and all the world will see Jesus descend on a cloud, angels reaping a harvest, and demons pouring out the fury of their hearts. The invisible war in heaven will be made tangible by a lovesick Bride rending the heavens with songs of longing to her groom on the other side of the heavenly veil, and the press of love will break the veil bit by bit...it really will. When the Bride becomes united in longing for her groom to return, she will simultaneously become united with God in His desire to be back on the garden He called "very good".   Jesus said when that happens, His glory would be seen on earth, because it is then that world will KNOW...not just believe...He is God's Son! This will all happen in a dangerous time, a time of trouble, that Jesus doesn't want His Bride "taken out of," but rather "kept through."

In John 17, Jesus lays out this strategy. Here, in one of the final prayers Jesus prays for His Bride, we hear God declare to God what will happen...in OUR generation:

John 17:15-24 I do not pray that You should take them out of the world, but that You should keep them from the evil one. They are not of the world, just as I am not of the world. (The Bride is staying as Jesus ministered to the lost and broken, so will she) ***Sanctify them by Your truth*** (she will be sanctified, or set apart from the world). ***Your word is truth. As You sent Me into the world, I also have sent them into the world. And for their sakes I sanctify Myself*** (just as Jesus was in the world, but not of it), ***that they also may be sanctified by the truth. "I do not pray for these alone, but also for those who will believe in Me through their word*** (Jesus declared this over YOU!)***; that they all may be one, as You, Father, are in Me, and I in You; that they also may be one in Us, that the world may believe that You sent Me*** (when all of the Bride shares the same desire of God, for Genesis 1:31 "very good" to be restored, God with man on earth, this process will open heaven)***. And the glory which You gave Me I have given them, that they may be one just as We are one*** (glory is light, we will be prepared in light to receive the brightness of Jesus coming)***: I in them, and You in Me; that they may be made perfect in one, and that the world may know that You have sent Me*** (heaven will open full and the world will see the King of Kings for who He is)***, and have loved them as You have loved Me.***

"Father, I desire that they also whom You gave Me may be with Me where I am, that they may behold My glory which You have given Me; for You loved Me before the foundation of the world. (Jesus is coming here...It is here, on earth, that we will behold His glory, Just as Adam and Eve lived in the bright light of God!)

David's Key is Jesus' Plan
This is the divine strategy for Jesus to return: that His entire Bride would use the key of David to unlock heaven. This is the generation that responds, or the Psalm 24 "Generation of Jacob." They will respond by being worshiping warriors, like David. The ancient gates that will open ARE the veil between heaven and earth:

Psalms 24:3-10 Who may ascend into the hill of the Lord ? Or who may stand in His holy place? He who has clean hands and a pure heart, Who has not lifted up his soul to an idol, Nor sworn deceitfully. He shall receive blessing from the Lord , And righteousness from the God of his salvation. This is Jacob, the generation of those who seek Him, Who seek Your face. Selah Lift up your heads, O you gates! And be lifted up, you everlasting doors! And the King of glory shall come in. Who is this King of glory? The Lord strong and mighty, The Lord mighty in battle. Lift up your heads, O you gates! Lift up, you everlasting doors! And the King of glory shall come in. Who is this King of glory? The Lord of hosts, He is the King of glory. Selah

It is David's Key of expressing night and day desire that unlocks the ancient gates in a process of corporate worship that will be found in each geographic area that responds! God sees the Churches of cities, not denominations or congregations per se. But, because mankind was given dominion of the very earth: the dirt, the rocks, the fishes, and the trees, God sees us geographically as we represent the places we live.

Genesis 1:27-28 So God created man in His own image; in the image of God He created him; male and female He created them. Then God blessed them, and God said to them, "Be fruitful and multiply; fill the earth and subdue it; have dominion over the fish of the sea, over the birds of the air, and over every living thing that moves on the earth."

David made worship and prayer...day and night...His entire governmental strategy over His patch of ground given to him to tend. This unlocked heaven in the most dramatic, but introductory, way! David hired 24,000 governmental workers to administer his government in Jerusalem. 8,000 people, or one third of his entire governmental staff, were dedicated to keep worship going day and night in Jerusalem. David made the worship center, called the house of the Lord, His governmental headquarters!:

I Chronicles 23:4-5 Of these, twenty-four thousand were to look after the work of the house of the Lord , six thousand were officers and judges, four thousand were gatekeepers, and four thousand praised the Lord with musical instruments, "which I made," said David, "for giving praise."

The music never stopped:

I Chronicles 9:33 These are the singers, heads of the fathers' houses of the Levites, who lodged in the chambers, and were free from other duties; for they were employed in that work day and night.

The music never stopped because the PRAYER never stopped! David's governmental philosophy was this: "why try to run this place without God? God wants to be here as much as we desperately need Him here. Why don't we express our desire to Him as our main activity, and He will give us all the rest!" Seeking God first is what Jesus said unlocks "all the rest" (Matthew 6). David believed this concept, put it into practical expression, and it worked!

Heaven Opens in a Process
Under David, the land was blessed. Israel didn't suffer invasion during David's reign, but rather went out and took new territory. By the time Solomon took the throne from David and placed the 24-hour worship in a permanent building called the temple, the Bible says the economy was prospering to such a degree that "gold was as common as silver and silver as common as stone." The agriculture changed as cedars became as common as sycamores...in less than 60 years even the

trees became more prosperous! This next passage describes heaven opening in the initial stages:

II Chronicles 1:14-15 And Solomon gathered chariots and horsemen; he had one thousand four hundred chariots and twelve thousand horsemen, whom he stationed in the chariot cities and with the king in Jerusalem. Also the king made silver and gold as common in Jerusalem as stones, and he made cedars as abundant as the sycamores which are in the lowland.

The healing of the land, the economic prosperity, and the protection from enemies were great benefits of heaven opening, but what David most desired was to "be with God where He was." When David prayed Psalm 27:4 and asked God to let him "inquire in the temple", there had never been a Jewish temple on earth. David was declaring to God, "I desire your company more than anything else, even all the benefits and power of ruling as king!" According to 1 Chronicles 29, God gave David the plans to build a worship center. That tabernacle released heaven on earth PRIMARILY through the Spirit of Prophecy, or the release of the Holy Spirit, in a tangible way.

The Psalms, by far, contain the most prophetic information in the Bible up to the point in time they were written, which was primarily David's generation. In a little more than 40 years, at least 95 of the 150 Psalms were written in David's 24-hour tabernacle worship movement.

"To the Chief Musician, a Psalm of David."

This is how David's government worked: the man after God's own heart saw a need in the land, he wrote a prayer, and handed it to the worship leader on duty. The worship leader sang it out, the military advisor's agreed, and God moved. Can you imagine?! You need to, because this is how the Bride will endure the final shaking of all things!

Look at who was working in the tabernacle worship prophesying with instruments! The very writers of the Psalms! Can you imagine how they started the tabernacle? I picture them saying something like "David, can't we sing the old songs we are good at?" David would respond "no, this isn't about music, this is about getting information from God! This is about increasing HIS government on earth!"

1 Chronicles 25:1-2 Moreover David and the captains of the army separated for the service some of the sons of Asaph, of Heman, and of Jeduthun, who should prophesy with harps, stringed instruments, and cymbals. And the number of the skilled men performing their service was: Of the sons of Asaph: Zaccur, Joseph, Nethaniah, and Asharelah; the sons of Asaph were under the direction of Asaph, who <u>prophesied according to the order of the king.</u>

These were the guys who authored MANY of the Psalms! They were ordered to prophesy...that was their job! The indwelling Spirit had not been given to mankind yet, David used the strategy given from heaven to go up to the heavens with desire. This is how the heavens are rent with love!! This is what Jesus describes as "spiritual violence": setting yourself apart, and setting your gaze on the one who WANTS to break in with power. This is what the earth is groaning for in our generation! If only an intentional and unified invitation will rise up from a patch of ground given to mankind!! If David and his men did this BEFORE the Spirit fell, what is possible now? Do we have a vision for it?!

Matthew 11:12 And from the days of John the Baptist until now the kingdom of heaven suffers violence, and the violent take it by force.

The violence of worship will literally tear the veil, and the light that comes through from heaven will heal the land once and for all.
Right now, all over the earth, Jesus is raising up a worship movement of night and day intercession that WILL open heaven. This is what He has always promised in His Word. The places where people agree are the strongholds...the Holy Mountains...the rocks set on high...that will keep God's companies of worshiping warriors not out of the world, but kept from the trouble, in the final shaking.
Can you feel the trembling? Can you see the storm? Night and day worship...the upper room tarrying for power...is what is required to bring in the final harvest in the most intense season earth has ever seen. This is what the angels, who will be seen and heard by the Bride opening heaven by rending the heavens with songs of love, declare in Revelation 14:

Revelation 14:6-12 Then I saw another angel flying in the midst of heaven, having the everlasting gospel to preach to those who dwell on the earth to every nation, tribe, tongue, and people—saying with a loud voice, "Fear God and give glory to Him, for the hour of His judgment has come; and worship Him who made heaven and earth, the sea and springs of water." And another angel followed, saying, "Babylon is fallen, is fallen, that great city, because she has made all nations drink of the wine of the wrath of her fornication." Then a third angel followed them, saying with a loud voice, "If anyone worships the beast and his image, and receives his mark on his forehead or on his hand, he himself shall also drink of the wine of the wrath of God, which is poured out full strength into the cup of His indignation. He shall be tormented with fire and brimstone in the presence of the holy angels and in the presence of the Lamb. And the smoke of their torment ascends forever and ever; and they have no rest day or night, who worship the beast and his image, and whoever receives the mark of his name." Here is the patience of the saints; here are those who keep the commandments of God and the faith of Jesus.

The Shepherds Will Go First

Jeremiah 3:15 And I will give you shepherds according to My heart, who will feed you with knowledge and understanding.

David is the "man after God's own heart." Right now, in this hour, Jeremiah 3:15 is being fulfilled. God is raising up shepherds after the heart of David who will lead the Bride into a worshiping war. These are the prophesied shepherds after God's own heart. Listen to them! Take what they tell you and search the Word! Is it true? If so, now is the time to build with everything.

These end time Davidic shepherds are the ones with the vision to build the end time cities of refuge where heaven will open, peace will flourish, resources will be abundant, and God will speak with clarity, just like David's generation experienced. Night and Day worship and prayer IS Jesus end time plan for the Bride. This will create a global "upper room" where the first harvesters will tarry for the power to go out and save a multitude without number. This is where you want to be when the shaking goes to a level far worse than what we are even seeing now.

Amos 9:9-12 "For surely I will command, And will sift the house of Israel among all nations, As grain is sifted in a sieve; Yet not the smallest grain shall fall to the ground. All the sinners of My people shall die by the sword, Who say, 'The calamity shall not overtake nor confront us.' "On that day I will raise up The tabernacle of David, which has fallen down, And repair its damages; I will raise up its ruins, And rebuild it as in the days of old; That they may possess the remnant of Edom, And all the Gentiles who are called by My name," Says the LORD who does this thing.

The Process is the Point

Jesus will sit on David's Throne. That makes David's story super important, especially in the hour Jesus is in the process of taking His place on earth. Listen, Jesus is coming to the climax in the process He has been leading for 6,000 years. Many of us wrongly believe that soon Jesus will suddenly "suspend" THAT process, get tired of all the sin, wave His hand, and make the earth right...suddenly...outside of the process that was written long ago and He has been executing patiently. This is absolutely NOT what the Bible says.

God LOVES the process. He designed the beautifully brilliant processes of every system of the earth...the water cycle, photosynthesis, tectonic plate movements, ocean currents...just look at the weather! How much MORE does God love the process of redemption He has planned and begun. He who began this good work in you is faithful to complete it.

God is not going to change the nature of what HE loves to satisfy mankind's impatience and unwillingness to do THEIR part of the process. Our part is super important, since it is OUR redemption. Jesus WILL partner with mankind in His return. The real question is: "will you partner with Jesus?" Because God gave man dominion on the earth, He refuses to operate on the earth apart from mankind.

Ezekiel 22:30-31 So I sought for a man among them who would make a wall, and stand in the gap before Me on behalf of the land, that I should not destroy it; but I found no one. Therefore I have poured out My indignation on them; I have consumed them with the fire of My wrath; and I have recompensed their deeds on their own heads," says the Lord GOD.

Satan also must find a man to agree, because God refuses to quit honoring the governmental authority He designed man for in the earth. That is why angels battle in the mid-heavens over the earth. There is a war being waged for the hearts of mankind to determine who will rule creation from earth. We know the end of the story, God WILL prevail.

Satan, a created usurper, could never beat the uncreated God! It isn't even a fair fight. There is an INFINITE unbalance of power between created Satan and his UNCREATED maker. BUT, God is unwilling to battle for the earth apart from mankind, whom He gave earth to. THAT is why the process has taken so long. THAT is why David's story is so important. David understood His role in the eternal government and God's role. Understanding the hour we live in, and what is REQUIRED of God's people is so important. There is great confusion in the camp of the Bride.

Jesus will partner with His spouse in the final hour, and she will prepare the earth for glory by incrementally becoming glorious (that means bright spotless light) like her Groom. The increasing power and glory of the Bride will adjust the eyes of the earth to receive Jesus.

THIS PROCESS IS INTENSE. Those who participate will offend the world. Light is very offensive to darkness, because light DESTROYS darkness.

John 1:9-10 That was the true Light which gives light to every man coming into the world. He was in the world, and the world was made through Him, and the world did not know Him.

Not only did the world not know Him...it hated the light!

John 3:19-21 And this is the condemnation, that the light has come into the world, and men loved darkness rather than light, because their deeds were evil. For everyone practicing evil hates the light and does not come to the light, lest his deeds should be exposed. But he who does the truth comes to the light, that his deeds may be clearly seen, that they have been done in God."

Not only did those who hate the light not come to the light, they tried to put out the light:

John 15:19-20 If you were of the world, the world would love its own. Yet because you are not of the world, but I chose you out of the world, therefore the world hates you. Remember the word that I said to you, 'A servant is not greater than his master.' If they persecuted Me, they will also persecute you. If they kept My word, they will keep yours also.

The Truth of Tribulation

Light coming into the darkness, and darkness resisting, is what we call "tribulation." Tribulation MUST accompany the coming of the kingdom, because the kingdom is ruled by a very bright man coming into the darkness the world mostly loves. That is why John said "if you want the kingdom of Jesus, then you want the tribulation of Jesus, which requires the patience of Jesus." You get all three together:

Revelation 1:9 I, John, both your brother and companion in the tribulation and kingdom and patience of Jesus Christ, was on the island that is called Patmos for the word of God and for the testimony of Jesus Christ.

Jesus is going to partner with mankind through tribulation. Jesus, the One who will sit on David's throne, is going to have musicians and gatekeepers running His global government, just like David had 24,000 musicians and gatekeepers running his government in Israel. This is what we call "night and day prayer to music" or the Tabernacle of David. The question is really "how many will partner with Him?!" Many will resist Him.

Luke 18:7-8 And shall God not avenge His own elect who cry out day and night to Him, though He bears long with them? I tell you that He will avenge them speedily. Nevertheless, when the Son of Man comes, will He really find faith on the earth?"

Tribulation Will Necessitate Vengeance

If you believe you will not be here for Jesus' return, or that he will show up in the sky any minute, or that He would never make you walk through trouble, then you are NOT planning on partnering with the Jesus of the Bible in His return. You really need to understand the nature of His government, the Bride He is coming back to, and the condition of the earth just before He breaks in with VICTORY.

The whole Bride will be one with Jesus in the final hours of victory over sin. To be chosen to live into the hour of victory is one of the hugest blessings available to mankind! But, many in the Church are hoping to be somewhere else! Will they be a part of the Bride?

Can you imagine a loving spouse blithely saying "Honey, I love you and all, I just think we are better off apart when you do the hard stuff"...what kind of marriage is that?! The truth is, Jesus carries the Bride THROUGH the hard stuff. The reluctance of believers to want to see the moment of Jesus' greatest victory, and the moment our love matures the most, is rooted in unbelief. We only wouldn't want to be there if we were unsure of two basic principles:

1. that the Groom WOULD BE victorious over the powers of hell,

or

2. That He really loved us and wanted the best for us.

Pre-tribulation vs. postribulation vs. no tribulation isn't a theology problem, it is a faith problem.

Unless you agree with the state of the world right now (surely you do not) Tribulation MUST happen, because a massive disruption of evil MUST happen. Don't you want to be here to see evil finally dealt with? I hope you do, because if you don't, you don't agree with Jesus' plans and you really need to search His heart, and yours.

Jesus refuses to violate love. That means he refuses to violate free will. Love requires free will. Therefore, Jesus has chosen to use the least intense means necessary to get the greatest number of people to agree with the coming of light at the deepest heart level, without ever violating the free will of the people of the earth. THAT is what the Revelation of Jesus Christ is describing.

Jesus is looking for voluntary lovers who love His appearing more than their own lives. Those who do will speak truth to authority despite the cost, operate in increasing signs and wonders, and increasing light. Many will be drawn to the light, and many will hate the light. What started in Jerusalem in 32 AD is not changing...it is MATURING...globally...and you HAVE A HUGE ROLE...if you want it. Everyone must choose.

2 Timothy 4:7-8 I have fought the good fight, I have finished the race, I have kept the faith. Finally, there is laid up for me the crown of righteousness, which the Lord, the righteous Judge, will give to me on that Day, and not to me only but also to all who have loved His appearing.

I hear the Lord say "to understand what is coming and what I desire, you must understand:
   1. who I am,
   2. what I have always done, and
   3. where I will rule from."

A Priest and a King
Jesus is a Priest and KING...like David...in the order of Melchizedek:

Psalms 110:1-4 A Psalm of David. The LORD said to my Lord,"Sit at My right hand, Till I make Your enemies Your footstool." The LORD shall send the rod of Your strength out of Zion. Rule in the midst of Your enemies! Your people shall be volunteers In the day of Your power; In the beauties of holiness, from the womb of the morning, You have the dew of Your youth. The LORD has sworn And will not relent, "You are a priest forever According to the order of Melchizedek."

Jesus has always done this: voluntarily submitted to the Father in love. Like David desired, Jesus perfectly did nothing in His own strength, instead, making His conversation with the Father (prayer) His source of strength as He obeyed every word of the Father:

Matthew 4:3-4 Now when the tempter came to Him, he said, "If You are the Son of God, command that these stones become bread." But He answered and said, "It is written, 'MAN SHALL NOT LIVE BY BREAD ALONE, BUT BY EVERY WORD THAT PROCEEDS FROM THE MOUTH OF GOD.' "

John 5:19-20 Then Jesus answered and said to them, "Most assuredly, I say to you, the Son can do nothing of Himself, but what He sees the Father do; for whatever He does, the Son also does in like manner. For the Father loves the Son, and shows Him all things that He Himself does; and He will show Him greater works than these, that you may marvel.

Jesus will rule from David's throne. That means, as David governed (as king) from a place of night and day intercession (priestly service), so will Jesus on earth (as He already does in heaven). David made night and day intercession the strength of Israel and became the greatest king Israel ever had, up until Jesus. Jesus didn't come to do away with the temple worship, which was supposed to be night and day, He came to CLEANSE the temple worship. Jesus is returning to a Bride who agrees with Him about night and day prayer, or a literal constant ABIDING conversation with God as a community, as the source of government in the earth. A priest AND king government. That is what we are in the process of watching happen before our eyes:

Luke 1:31-32 And behold, you will conceive in your womb and bring forth a Son, and shall call His name JESUS. He will be great, and will be called the Son of the Highest; and the Lord God will give Him the throne of His father David.

Matthew 21:12-14 Then Jesus went into the temple of God and drove out all those who bought and sold in the temple, and overturned the tables of the money changers and the seats of those who sold doves. And He said to them, "It is written, 'MY HOUSE SHALL BE CALLED A HOUSE OF PRAYER,' but you have made it a 'DEN OF THIEVES.'" Then the blind and the lame came to Him in the temple, and He healed them.

Jesus didn't leave the temple, but rather cleansed it that glory...manifested in this Matthew 21 passage in healing power...would come to earth. This is what His Father told Him to do! God is not done with temple worship. He is coming to cleanse and rebuild it in the manner David did, so the glory can come.

Because the men of the earth hate the light, or glory, of Jesus' absolute reign, there is a storm coming as people resist Jesus' process of returning! The Bible is CLEAR about this. This is really simple. For the last 2,000 years a storm has been building like a big hurricane. Some may get confused because smaller "thunder storms" (like the destruction of Jerusalem in 70 AD) have been in front of the hurricane, but believe me, THE storm that is coming will result in Jesus' physical presence on earth at the end of 7 years...period. THAT storm has never come. It did not come in 70 AD. To tell people the intense events that are warned of over and over in the Bible have already happened is the same as telling them to not prepare for the very thing Jesus warned of over and over! Woe to anyone who believes the complicated reckoning of man over the simple and straightforward warnings of the Bible.

Daniel 12:1-7 "At that time Michael shall stand up, The great prince who stands watch over the sons of your people; And there shall be a time of trouble, Such as never was since there was a nation, Even to that time. And at that time your people shall be delivered, Every one who is found written in the book. And many of those who sleep in the dust of the earth shall awake, Some to everlasting life, Some to shame and everlasting contempt. Those who are wise shall shine Like the brightness of the firmament, And those who turn many to righteousness Like the stars forever and ever. "But you, Daniel, shut up the words, and seal the book until the time of the end; many shall run to and fro, and knowledge shall increase." Then I, Daniel, looked; and there stood two others, one on this riverbank and the other on that riverbank. And one said to the man clothed in linen, who was above the waters of the river, "How long shall the fulfillment of these wonders be? " Then I heard the man clothed in linen, who was above the waters of the river, when he held up his right hand and his left hand to heaven, and swore by Him who lives forever, that it shall be for a time, times, and half a time; and when the power of the holy

people has been completely shattered, all these things shall be finished.

A storm IS coming and the Bible has already generated a forecast and model of the nature, scope and size of this storm. What we are seeing in the world is matching the forecasted storm track to a "t," and though it hasn't made landfall just yet, the wind and waves are already lashing much of the earth.

Right now, the American Church happens to live in a poorly constructed tower on a hill. Though the tower was made well, we have intentionally dug out the foundation stones and filled in the holes with sand. This generation of believers is being bullied into feeling guilty for how firm the Church stands on one man and what He has said is true, as if that were too exclusive. This is the problem with this line of thinking: truth only occupies one place. There are an infinite number of places of falsity, but each true thing has only one place it is found. This country, founded on truth, has been trading truths for lies. Woe

Isaiah 5:20-21 Woe to those who call evil good, and good evil; Who put darkness for light, and light for darkness; Who put bitter for sweet, and sweet for bitter! Woe to those who are wise in their own eyes, And prudent in their own sight!

The heat of passionate devotion to Jesus has been watered down with cooler...more palatable philosophies of tolerance. Lukewarm will not endure the end time events (Revelation 3:16). When the storm comes, this corrupted ... this lukewarm ... house will be spit out. Anyone who tells you differently is lying to you. There is an answer to the storm, but those lying to you in order to keep you happy are actually creating the conditions of your destruction. That is what Matthew 7 is all about. That is why the Bible says this about the most luxurious country to ever inhabit the planet:

Revelation 18:2-8 And he cried mightily with a loud voice, saying, "Babylon the great is fallen, is fallen, and has become a dwelling place of demons, a prison for every foul spirit, and a cage for every unclean and hated bird! For all the nations have drunk of the wine of the wrath of her fornication, the kings of the earth have committed fornication with her, and the merchants of the earth have become rich through the abundance of her luxury." And I heard another voice from heaven saying, "Come out of her, my people, lest you share in her sins, and lest you receive of her plagues. For her sins have reached to heaven, and God has remembered her iniquities. Render to her just as she rendered to you, and repay her double according to her works; in the cup which she has mixed, mix double for her. In the measure that she glorified herself and lived luxuriously, in the same measure give her torment and sorrow; for she says in her heart, 'I sit as queen, and am no widow, and will not see sorrow.' Therefore her plagues will come in one day—death and mourning and famine. And she will be utterly burned with fire, for strong is the Lord God who judges her.

There is only one country who fits the bill of this passage, and the hundreds of others, about end time Babylon. The USA was once the Golden City of Isaiah 14, and has now become a haunt of demons.

Spend a minute to consider this Revelation 18 passage. Ask yourself: Do we not export more lust and materialistic dreams than any other? Do not the kings of the earth court us for their own influence to grow? Do we not sit in excess waste and luxury while much of the world scratches the soil for their daily bread? Have we not systematically ruled God out of our foundations and found demons of murder, theft, violence, and lust rushing into every gaping hole God once filled? Do you watch the news? This is plain to see. Our children plot to mass murder each other on almost a monthly basis! Our workers hate their coworkers and their own lives so much that they store up weapons to kill as many as possible. We ASSUME our politicians are corrupt! We condone, if not participate in, theft, greed, lust...we are the haunt of demons spoken of in Revelation 18...how could we not see this?

This is where David comes into the story again. Few preach the Biblical solution to America's corruption, preferring to blindly grope and declare revival sans active community repentance. The prescription of God is to not "look on the bright side, and proclaim falsely that revival is coming to the nation" as the false prophets of our day will tell you. It is simply not. The prescription is what David did when His sin was found out: agree with God!

II Samuel 12:15-17 Then Nathan departed to his house. And the Lord struck the child that Uriah's wife bore to David, and it became ill. David therefore pleaded with God for the child, and David fasted and went in and lay all night on the ground. So the elders of his house arose and went to him, to raise him up from the ground. But he would not, nor did he eat food with them.

God says Babylon is fallen because of her excessive corruption and luxury. The Church keeps lying and saying Babylon is on the verge of revival. Only one of us can be right, and I am pretty sure it is God. Once you agree with God, you MUST come out of the false thinking that got you into the very trouble that God used to wake you up. Now is not the time to arrogantly proclaim your own theology that revival is coming to every nation BEFORE Jesus sets up His throne in Jerusalem! That will never actually produce the promised Joel 2 revival! What produces the revival we need is the "tearing of the heart."

Now is the time to agree with the Bible...come out of rebellious thinking before it is too late, because a huge storm is really coming.

OK, Tom. How do I come out?

It is simple: You trade the American dream (of having a good life in the next 10 to 30 years) and the American governmental hope of someone coming along...a human "king"... to fix your problems, and instead put on Jesus' dream (to be back in His garden) as your main priority, and Jesus' government (being enthroned on the praises of His people night and day) as your only hope. This will actually produce the first fruits of His government, which we call...drum roll please....revival!

Right now, our sin is found out. Much of the Church couldn't honestly care less. The level of apathy about the world being on fire is actually sickening. Few even watch the news. The American Church is so lukewarm we are about to be vomited out. As long as most western Christians can find someone to give them a "good word", they go on blindly believing revival is coming to Babylon. Revival WILL come to the places that repent IN Babylon, but transferring your responsibility to contend for your own city onto a patriotic ideal of national revival is actually disagreeing with God, and setting YOUR city up for a massive fall.

Let me be clear: Jesus does not want us to infiltrate and take back the government of the USA, any more than he instructed Peter, James, or Paul to run for the Roman Senate! Despite what most Church leaders will tell you, we are supposed to do what Christians have always been supposed to do, separate (sanctify) ourselves, be united in warning the world of the coming judgment, and preach the good news that life starts when the real king arrives and sets up His throne in Jerusalem, where David ruled:

John 17:15-21 I do not pray that You should take them out of the world, but that You should keep them from the evil one. They are not of the world, just as I am not of the world. Sanctify them by Your truth. Your word is truth. As You sent Me into the world, I also have sent them into the world. And for their sakes I sanctify Myself, that they also may be sanctified by the truth. "I do not pray for these alone, but also for those who will believe in Me through their word; that they all may be one, as You, Father, are in Me, and I in You; that they also may be one in Us, that the world may believe that You sent Me.

Jesus looked at His best friends and called us all a part of them! Whatever those guys and gals did, so should we. They didn't have a seven mountain mandate, they had a great commission. Jesus WILL conquer every mountain, but He wants to do it with us, in a real time conversation! Those friends of Jesus understood the cost of simply unplugging from Jesus' instructions and, in arrogance, doing things FOR Jesus. After the resurrection, they understood the need to simply obey Jesus, in real time. Going into an upper room and "praying until" really worked! Look at Acts 5. They didn't infiltrate the world! Their desire DIVIDED the world, and those who wanted truth infiltrated them! What started in Jerusalem will cover the globe, but how many will agree with this plan:

Acts 5:11-29 So great fear came upon all the church and upon all who heard these things. And through the hands of the apostles many signs and wonders were done among the people. And they were all with one accord in Solomon's Porch. Yet none of the rest dared join them, but the people esteemed them highly. And believers were increasingly added to the Lord, multitudes of both men and women, so that they brought the sick out into the streets and laid them on beds and couches, that at least the shadow of Peter passing by might fall on some of them. Also a multitude gathered from the surrounding cities to Jerusalem, bringing sick people and those who were tormented by unclean spirits, and they were all healed.

Then the high priest rose up, and all those who were with him (which is the sect of the Sadducees), and they were filled with indignation, and laid their hands on the apostles and put them in the common prison. But at night an angel of the Lord opened the prison doors and brought them out, and said, "Go, stand in the temple and speak to the people all the words of this life."

And when they heard that, they entered the temple early in the morning and taught. But the high priest and those with him came and called the council together, with all the elders of the children of Israel, and sent to the prison to have them brought. But when the officers came and did not find them in the prison, they returned and reported, saying, "Indeed we found the prison shut securely, and the guards standing outside before the doors; but when we opened them, we found no one inside!" Now when the high priest, the captain of the temple, and the chief priests heard these things, they wondered what the outcome would be. So one came and told them, saying, "Look, the men whom you put in prison are standing in the temple and teaching the people!"

Then the captain went with the officers and brought them without violence, for they feared the people, lest they should be stoned. And when they had brought them, they set them before the council. And the high priest asked them, saying, "Did we not strictly command you not to teach in this name? And look, you have filled Jerusalem with your doctrine, and intend to bring this Man's blood on us!" But Peter and the other apostles answered and said: "We ought to obey God rather than men.

This is the heart of a lovesick Bride who doesn't want the world made better by Jesus, but will not settle for anything less than a world RULED by Jesus...for real. This was David's heart lived out in community.

Rejoining Heaven and Earth Under One King

David "took much trouble" to prepare to build the temple. The Bible says David, rather than build his fortune on earth, spent what he had on getting ready for God's house to be built, so that the music and prayer would never stop on earth. This is really important, because Jesus is in the process of joining heaven back to earth:

Ephesians 1:9-10 having made known to us the mystery of His will, according to His good pleasure which He purposed in Himself, that in the dispensation of the fullness of the times He might gather together in one all things in Christ, both which are in heaven and which are on earth—in Him.

Heaven and earth ARE coming back together. Soon. Mankind has a huge role in this. The earth was given to mankind, who are supposed to extend God's government over said earth. Man in partnership with God. This, according to God, is very good. When Adam and Eve rebelled against God's leadership, for love, God separated heaven from earth. That was NOT good. But, heaven joined to earth, and more importantly, man joined to God, is what God called "very good" at the time of creation. The Bible documents that God has a plant plan to get what He wants!

Man is supposed to be partnering with Jesus in re-connecting heaven and earth. Right now, our job is to get as many people as want to be in God's family reconnected to the family, so that God can begin renewing the physical earth in great glory. Our job STARTS with power from on high, tarrying night and day in "upper rooms" all over the earth until the power comes...bit by bit...and then taking the next measure, to grow the kingdom the next bit. This process builds until Jesus has His family ready to receive Him in all His GLORY! This place He will return to is called His throne, which is His governmental position as head of His body on earth.

Glory is the bright light of God's presence. Right now, we are stuck with the dim light of the sun that barely keeps earth going until God returns. The return of God's glory to earth will destroy any darkness. In order to endure the re-appearance of God on earth, mankind must choose: "will I be led by Jesus, the light of Mankind, and live forever in the source-light of life, or do I want to be led by darkness and forever exist in a state of non-life?"

Jesus sent His disciples out to extend this good news: that life, if you want it, is now available. When the earth is prepared, called the harvest time, Jesus will return to the throne WE build for Him, and begin remaking the earth. That is called the end of the age:

Matthew 28:18-20 And Jesus came and spoke to them, saying, "All authority has been given to Me in heaven and on earth. Go therefore and make disciples of all the nations, baptizing them in the name of the Father and of the Son and of the Holy Spirit, teaching them to observe all things that I have commanded you; and lo, I am with you always, even to the end of the age." Amen.

God has His part in this process, and mankind has OUR part in this process. David understood this and began doing His part. Jesus told His disciples what David already knew: mankind is supposed to pray privately, but also corporately, as their PRIMARY activity. Specifically, this is to be our desire:

Matthew 6:10 Your kingdom come. Your will be done On earth as it is in heaven.

Right now, in heaven, worship and intercession is happening 24/7/356. As David cried out for God to be His one desire, God showed David how to make earth agree with heaven, and David obeyed God and built the worship movement God showed him. God showed David to make the worship movement that never stopped the center of David's government. When David told everything to Solomon in order to pass the baton, he told Solomon "this is all God's idea, not mine!"

1 Chronicles 28:19 "All this," said David, "the LORD made me understand in writing, by His hand upon me, all the works of these plans."

David paved the way for us to understand what is required of US. David saw HIS part as spending His desire...asking with his words, for God to be with him. This agreed with what God desires, and God did amazing things to advance His own desires on earth THROUGH David's invitation. That is why Jesus said ask, seek, and knock. It is extending the invitation to God to break in to our lives, our city, and our earth that open the gates for Him to come in:

Matthew 7:7-11 "Ask, and it will be given to you; seek, and you will find; knock, and it will be opened to you. For everyone who asks receives, and he who seeks finds, and to him who knocks it will be opened. Or what man is there among you who, if his son asks for bread, will give him a stone? Or if he asks for a fish, will he give him a serpent? If you then, being evil, know how to give good gifts to your children, how much more will your Father who is in heaven give good things to those who ask Him!

David began asking as his ONE desire, and the more David spent himself, the more revelation he got.   This became the passion of David's life. David said he spent all he had on the seeking of God to be with him. David sought God with the whole heart, and taught others to do the same.

Psalms 119:2 Blessed are those who keep His testimonies, Who seek Him with the whole heart!

The more David spent himself on God, the more God gave him. This is the irony of wholeheartedness: spending all your heart, soul, mind, and strength on God is a REALLY good deal for you! The more you try to spend your life on God, the more life He gives you! The one trying to live the most "spent" often appears from the outside to have too much! This is the mystery of God's economy. Jesus brings life in full. David told Solomon "the more I set apart for God, the more abundant the gold and silver became! I couldn't out give Him":

I Chronicles 22:14-16 Indeed I have taken much trouble to prepare for the house of the Lord one hundred thousand talents of gold and one million talents of silver, and bronze and iron beyond measure, for it is so abundant. I have prepared timber and stone also, and you may add to them. Moreover there are workmen with you in abundance: woodsmen and stonecutters, and all types of skillful men for every kind of work. Of gold and silver and bronze and iron there is no limit. Arise and begin working, and the Lord be with you."

God called David the man after His own heart. This is because David agreed with God that life is only "very good" when David and God are as close as possible. David knew that his only role in this equation was "spending his desire on God" and that God had the plans and strength to make it all work. David was not religious...David was lovesick. David understood that God desired to be with David where he was, too. This is confidence in love:

Psalms 27:8-10 When You said, "Seek My face," My heart said to You, "Your face, Lord , I will seek." Do not hide Your face from me; Do not turn Your servant away in anger; You have been my help; Do not leave me nor forsake me, O God of my salvation. When my father and my mother forsake me, Then the Lord will take care of me.

Jesus agrees with David:

Luke 14:26-28 "If anyone comes to Me and does not hate his father and mother, wife and children, brothers and sisters, yes, and his own life also, he cannot be My disciple. And whoever does not bear his cross and come after Me cannot be My disciple. For which of you, intending to build a tower, does not sit down first and count the cost, whether he has enough to finish it —

Jesus was clear that the only way to be His disciple is to love Him more than your own family...your own wife, husband, or kids...more than mom or dad. There is a practical reason behind this...it is the truth about love. The truth about love is this: there is no love apart from the love that emanates from God. God is the wellspring of love in creation. We can only love because God first loved us:

I John 4:19 We love Him because He first loved us.

That is what David is describing in Psalm 27..."God, I love you with everything...but you said 'seek my face' and I responded. I don't know where this whole thing started, but what I know is I am alive and safe with you!"

This is the heart condition that God calls very good. God desires voluntary lovers...not workers, not soldiers, not performers...voluntary lovesick sons and daughters, a Bride for His Son. If you spend your love, which is really obedience, on Him, even at the cost of your own family, He will lavish love back on you in such abundance it will cause you to love your family better! That is what it means to seek God first and have the rest added unto you.

This reality peaked for David when he realized that he was living in a nice permanent house, but the place set aside for God was a simple tent! The moment that David realized he was more settled on God's garden than God was, David desired to fix that. When David expressed this to God, he got the surprise of a lifetime! God told David that because this was the desire of David's heart, God would, in fact, build David a house, make him safe through any trouble that came, and set God's own Son on David's throne forever!

I Chronicles 17:3-14 But it happened that night that the word of God came to Nathan, saying, "Go and tell My servant David, 'Thus says the Lord : "You shall not build Me a house to dwell in. For I have not dwelt in a house since the time that I brought up Israel, even to this day, but have gone from tent to tent, and from one tabernacle to another. Wherever I have moved about with all Israel, have I ever spoken a word to any of the judges of Israel, whom I commanded to shepherd My people, saying, 'Why have you not built Me a house of cedar–' " ' Now therefore, thus shall you say to My servant David, 'Thus says the Lord of hosts: "I took you from the sheepfold, from following the sheep, to be ruler over My people Israel. And I have been with you wherever you have gone, and have cut off all your enemies from before you, and have made you a name like the name of the great men who are on the earth. Moreover I will appoint a place for My people Israel, and will plant them, that they may dwell in a place of their own and move no more; nor shall the sons of wickedness oppress them anymore, as previously, since the time that I commanded judges to be over My people Israel. Also I will subdue all your enemies. Furthermore I tell you that the Lord will build you a house. And it shall be, when your days are fulfilled, when you must go to be with your fathers, that I will set up your seed after you, who will be of your sons; and I will establish his kingdom. He shall build Me a house, and I will establish his throne forever. I will be his Father, and he shall be My son; and I will not take My mercy away from him, as I took it from him who was before you. And I will establish him in My house and in My kingdom forever; and his throne shall be established forever." ' "

God's Desire Should Be Our Vision

God made the earth for Himself. Jesus will reign on earth forever as a MAN, fully God, yet fully man, forever. It is only after Jesus returns to re-establish what God called "very good" in Genesis 1:31 that life will REALLY begin again for mankind. Right now we are in a partially dead state, though many of us are trying to make the best of our partial deadness, Jesus says "trade the partial deadness and spend yourself on me and I will give you LIFE IN FULL!" What is my life vision? How far does it extend. If I want to live for trillions of years, I really need to have a vision for how to practically live in that reality.

When you come into the realization that your are more settled into your life without God than you are zealous for Him to come back, you must respond to that emotion, like David did while living in his nice house. God is done waiting for the Bride to come to this realization herself and has begun the final strokes of a perfect plan to shake the Church into choosing one way or the other. We call this TRIBULATION. Many believers, in arrogance, will be offended by God's intense plan to get His Bride to choose, and will quit, according to the Bible.

Tribulation is already beginning. Christian persecution is skyrocketing in the Middle East and Asia. This is what will grow globally in the next months and years, as God withdraws his restraint from the evil in men's hearts in order to show us what life looks like on planet earth without His leadership, the people truly in love with God will MOURN that reality and press in like David. The lovesick will forgo their very plans and dreams to cry out to God day and night to break back into the garden with light. THIS is Jesus' plan as written in Revelation:

Revelation 6:9-11 When He opened the fifth seal, I saw under the altar the souls of those who had been slain for the word of God and for the testimony which they held. And they cried with a loud voice, saying, "How long, O Lord, holy and true, until You judge and avenge our blood on those who dwell on the earth?" Then a white robe was given

to each of them; and it was said to them that they should rest a little
while longer, until both the number of their fellow servants and their
brethren, who would be killed as they were, was completed.

On earth, the cry will be the same as in heaven. Heaven and
earth are going to begin joining in agreement day and night for Jesus to
break in to the garden and begin physically establishing HIS just
government on the earth. Simultaneously, the "best government ever
tried" will fail as socialistic solutions collapse one last time. The best
man-based government will hate Christians and kill them for giving their
loyalty to Jesus rather than the antichrist, who many will think can fix
the world:

David's Throne Will Crush The Antichrist's Government
To blaspheme is to slander something sacred, or to call what
God calls good, evil. The antichrist will blaspheme the Tabernacle of
David. He will call it evil for the glory it is releasing into the earth.

David's tabernacle is weird in our day. Many do not understand
or like the 24/7 prayer movement. It was odd in David's day, too. At
least we have David as an example. All David had was God's still small
voice moving His heart. David simply obeyed God in building this very
odd worship movement, because David LOVED God. If you love God,
you WILL obey Him over people. David's sons were probably not that
happy that dad took their inheritance and spent it all on a fairly small
building to house night and day worship! But David's obedience to God
moved God's heart powerfully and provided a rich inheritance for his
sons.

David's obedience to the odd plans of the invisible God re-
established in Jerusalem God's throne on earth THROUGH David's
throne, or office of power. When we talk about David's throne, we
aren't talking about the wooden chair David sat on, we are talking about
the place and nature of David's government. Jesus will govern the earth
WHERE and LIKE David did. David knew EXACTLY why 24/7 prayer was
so important, because it made a throne for God on earth:

Psalms 22:2-3 O My God, I cry in the daytime, but You do not hear;
And in the night season, and am not silent. But You are holy,
Enthroned in the praises of Israel.

David made a practical way for God to be enthroned on the praises of His people 24/7...continually...and God CAME and inhabited it. Jesus will govern the earth the same way!

Right now, we are in the initial stages of constructing a government that will overtake every existing government on earth. We aren't supposed to infiltrate the existing evil governments, but rather crush them by worshiping Jesus 24/7 until He comes to the new government which bridges the gaps between heaven and earth. Light is not supposed to vainly attempt to cooperate with darkness:

2 Corinthians 6:14 Do not be unequally yoked together with unbelievers. For what fellowship has righteousness with lawlessness? And what communion has light with darkness?

The throne Jesus is constructing through praise is a superior supernatural, yet-becoming-natural, government constructed entirely through voluntary desire. That desire is expressed through worship and intercession, and makes a space for Jesus to rule a people who want Him! 24/7 prayer is just starting on earth and will go on forever, as it is in heaven.

By building night and day prayer in this hour, we are actually constructing a superior government which will consume the existing lesser governments that can only temporarily control the earth. The antichrist empire that is emerging right now is nothing compared to the throne of David, but you will only enjoy the protection of the superior throne to the degree you agree with constructing it, for real. It is voluntary love that builds it, so you get as much of it as you want. Wanting it "all the way" puts you "all the way under it", which completely protects you from the efforts to resist it.

In Daniel 2, Daniel was shown the SUPERIORITY of the throne God would establish through praise. The fourth kingdom of Nebuchadnezzar's dream is the antichrist empire described as the feet of iron and clay (socialism and Islam) that extended out of the iron legs of the Ottoman Empire, or the Islamic Empire. At the same time the iron and clay temporarily mix, Jesus will begin constructing HIS throne, which we have already seen IS the throne of His ancestor, David. Look at what Daniel stated was God's interpretation of Nebuchadnezzar's dream:

Daniel 2:40-44 And the fourth kingdom shall be as strong as iron, inasmuch as iron breaks in pieces and shatters everything; and like iron that crushes, that kingdom will break in pieces and crush all the others. Whereas you saw the feet and toes, partly of potter's clay and partly of iron, the kingdom shall be divided; yet the strength of the iron shall be in it, just as you saw the iron mixed with ceramic clay. And as the toes of the feet were partly of iron and partly of clay, so the kingdom shall be partly strong and partly fragile. As you saw iron mixed with ceramic clay, they will mingle with the seed of men; but they will not adhere to one another, just as iron does not mix with clay. And in the days of these kings the God of heaven will set up a kingdom which shall never be destroyed; and the kingdom shall not be left to other people; it shall break in pieces and consume all these kingdoms, and it shall stand forever.

Right now, on earth, the Islamic caliphate is literally reviving, and as we see the feet grow out of the legs, it is mixing with a liberal socialist agenda, in the form of the Muslim Brotherhood partnering with the American political establishment! The liberal left of the world is uniting with political Islam in order to control the Middle East. The largest embassy in the world is the US embassy just outside of what was Babylon at the time Nebuchadnezzar got this dream. Policy makers who are for homosexual marriage and women's rights are literally partnering, by sending arms, money, and political cover, with those who literally hang homosexuals in the public square and make women "stay indoors as to not offend the culture." AT THE EXACT SAME TIME night and day prayer is beginning in hundreds, if not thousands, of locations globally. This is no accident friends, Jesus is about to return. There is so much to do! David's throne will be rebuilt, but what will your part be? Will Jesus find faith when He returns (Luke 18:8).

WATCH. PRAY. BE READY.

The New Song - 4

There is a very specific phrase in the Bible regarding the end-time worship movement that God will use to rebuild the Tabernacle of David, and hence, Jesus' Throne, prior to the return of the Lord. This end-time promise is called the "New Song." The New Song is for one generation. The Bible is actually quite clear about this. Doing a Word search for the phrase New Song will actually change the way you see the end times, IF you know what to look for.

God has promised to raise up night and day "worship to music," called "David's Tabernacle," as part of Jesus' plan to return and begin establishing His physical kingdom on earth. Jesus has a very specific plan He is executing right now, before our very eyes. They key point of involvement for Jesus' Bride is found in night and day worship. This isn't "another neat thing the Church is doing"...this is actually what everyone who is loyal to Jesus will be doing as their primary purpose as the return of Jesus draws near! It is just starting now, but by the time it as all said and done, Jesus' Church will be a seven day a week night and day worshiping and interceding Bride releasing judgment in the earth in real time!

There is SO much information in the Bible about this exact subject. Passages about how it happens, when it happens, why it happens, and how God will use the "New Song" to actually release judgment on earth. There are passages about what will result from this worship movement being built, what will happen in places that don't build it, what those who do not participate risk losing, what those who build it will gain. There is SO MUCH to do, and so much information about it. Every time Jesus spoke of His return He said "watch, pray, or be ready." You can only obey Jesus if you know what to watch for (not

Him appearing suddenly in the sky, as that requires no preparation, for every eye will see Him!), what to pray for, and how to BE READY!

Luke 12:40, 47-48 Therefore you also be ready, for the Son of Man is coming at an hour you do not expect." ...And that servant who knew his master's will, and did not prepare himself or do according to his will, shall be beaten with many stripes. But he who did not know, yet committed things deserving of stripes, shall be beaten with few. For everyone to whom much is given, from him much will be required; and to whom much has been committed, of him they will ask the more.

This is a sober warning Jesus gave HIS DISCIPLES! Jesus' plan is clear and plain. All of His disciples knew the plan. They saw it being worked out all around them: the praying day and night, the persecution, the martyrdom, the Church advancing under resistance, the signs, the wonders, the mass salvation. They KNEW what to watch for and they were seeing the beginning of it. That is why they said things like this:

I John 2:18 Little children, it is the last hour; and as you have heard that the Antichrist is coming, even now many antichrists have come, by which we know that it is the last hour.

But, very few people know the plan or these numerous passages, let alone teach them. There are over 150 Chapters in the Bible specifically regarding Jesus' return as the Lion, and only 89 Chapters describing Jesus' sacrifice as the Lamb...but mostly the Church doesn't talk about the Lion's plans! There is so much that can be uncovered. This message is being re-discovered in this hour. The original disciples knew this message well, and they lived it out: gathering together in one accord in the upper room, and seeing, in an introductory way, the results promised by the Word: the Spirit poured out, signs, wonders, miracles, and mass salvation. They literally witnessed everyone calling on the name of the Lord being saved in the thousands at a time. But, somehow, in the passage of time and the patience of the Lord, this message was forgotten.

In the western world, the Church became more comfortable, the resistance subsided. The Bride-to-be forgot what she once knew. In the 10/40 window, the Church has been living the first pangs of the last days (this was promised to the seven churches of revelation: that some would have 10 days of trouble instead of 7)...and it is coming here...like a freight train speeding down the tracks...but, oh how we have forgotten what those disciples knew. We have mostly lost vision for how they lived. John, the beloved who laid his head against Jesus breast, lived through tribulation. How can we receive Revelation from this best friend of our Beloved and still imagine we will see less trouble than he did? John opens his final statement to the Church with these words:

Revelation 1:9 I, John, both your brother and companion in the <u>tribulation</u> and <u>kingdom</u> and <u>patience</u> of Jesus Christ, was on the island that is called Patmos for the word of God and for the testimony of Jesus Christ.

Tribulation = Patience = Kingdom

John said I am his companion in three specific and glorious areas if I consider the Bible, including Revelation, to be MY TRUTH. What are those three areas?! The tribulation, the patience, and the kingdom of Jesus!

Like I said, the plans are clear, but we are so far removed from them that the Bride mostly doesn't know the plans of her Groom. But, they are written and easily re-discovered with the help of the Holy Spirit:

John 16:13-15 However, when He, the Spirit of truth, has come, He will guide you into all truth; for He will not speak on His own authority, but whatever He hears He will speak; and He will tell you things to come. He will glorify Me, for He will take of what is Mine and declare it to you. All things that the Father has are Mine. Therefore I said that He will take of Mine and declare it to you.

So I am going to mine out this idea of the "New Song" and see what it means for me, as a partner with John in the tribulation, the patience, and the kingdom of Jesus. If you know what to look for, you can see the New Song raising up globally, from coast to coast, sea to sea, and mountain to valley. This is what was promised to Isaiah in probably the most well-known passage concerning the New Song. Here we see clearly that the New Song is related to Jesus releasing end time judgment. This is one of the primary purposes of the New Song: for Jesus' spouse to agree with Him on earth for His desire to bring His kingdom from heaven, which requires driving everything that hinders love off of His garden (this is judgment):

Isaiah 42:10-17 (This is what the Bride does night and day):
Sing to the Lord a New Song, And His praise from the ends of the earth, You who go down to the sea, and all that is in it, You coastlands and you inhabitants of them! Let the wilderness and its cities lift up their voice, The villages that Kedar inhabits. Let the inhabitants of Sela sing, Let them shout from the top of the mountains. Let them give glory to the Lord , And declare His praise in the coastlands.

(This is what Jesus does in response):
The Lord shall go forth like a mighty man; He shall stir up His zeal like a man of war. He shall cry out, yes, shout aloud; He shall prevail against His enemies. "I have held My peace a long time, I have been still and restrained Myself. Now I will cry like a woman in labor, I will pant and gasp at once. I will lay waste the mountains and hills, And dry up all their vegetation; I will make the rivers coastlands, And I will dry up the pools. I will bring the blind by a way they did not know; I will lead them in paths they have not known. I will make darkness light before them, And crooked places straight. These things I will do for them, And not forsake them. They shall be turned back, They shall be greatly ashamed, Who trust in carved images, Who say to the molded images, 'You are our gods.'

God's Judgment is Set to Music

Every time the Bible uses the exact phrase "New Song", you will see it associated with the release of end-time judgment. There are nine uses of the exact phrase, but there are many more passages describing the judgments being released to music. The nine passages are: Psalm 33, 40, 96, 98, 144, 149, Isaiah 42, Revelation 5:9, and Revelation 14:3.

One of the most dramatic passages where judgment being released to the music of God's people is in Isaiah 30:

Isaiah 30:27-32 (GNT) The Lord's power and glory can be seen in the

distance. Fire and smoke show his anger. He speaks, and his words burn like fire. He sends the wind in front of him like a flood that carries everything away. It sweeps nations to destruction and puts an end to their evil plans. But you, God's people, will be happy and sing as you do on the night of a sacred festival. You will be as happy as those who walk to the music of flutes on their way to the Temple of the Lord, the defender of Israel. The Lord will let everyone hear his majestic voice and feel the force of his anger. There will be flames, cloudbursts, hailstones, and torrents of rain. The Assyrians will be terrified when they hear the Lord's voice and feel the force of his punishment. As the Lord strikes them again and again, his people will keep time with the music of drums and harps. God himself will fight against the Assyrians.

This is Jesus' plan, to war against everything that hinders love, by making war the way God has always made war... sending the worshipers first!

There are some amazing and very specific reasons God makes worship our warfare, but the easiest way I can think of to say it is this: God has given mankind dominion of the earth, but He says that He is our strength. This is what God called "very good." This is His desire: us subduing the earth and agreeing with Him about returning it to very good...longing for Eden with Him. As we do that verbally in the place of intercession, taking our place of dominion with our words, Jesus WILL begin to remove everything that hinders love using specific events. We call these events the Book of Revelation! The Book of Revelation isn't mostly negative! It is the story of the most amazing wedding to ever take place, and like every good wedding, the music...the New Song...is key!

The phrase "New Song" is talking about the end-time restoring of David's Tabernacle globally. The Bible is actually clear that the end-time 24/7 worship movement will be global. This is because Jesus is coming to "drive evil off the planet" globally. Wholehearted abandoned love for Jesus is a crucial element to this plan. The New Song, and the building of this night and day worship movement, is about whole-hearted love expressed in a practical way. Sincere love for Jesus is not the same as wholehearted love for Jesus!

David's Song Will Drive Away Evil

This idea of driving "evil" off the planet is really important to understand. Evil isn't a force equal and opposite to God that He needs to defeat in one last show of strength. Evil is actually VERY EASY for God to destroy, because evil isn't a force at all, but rather the absence of God. Inviting God with worship fills the void of His leadership.

God is the light...the power source, to use a crude analogy...for mankind. Evil is the absence of God's light. The Bible likens this to the relationship of dark to light. God is light, evil is darkness. Darkness is simply the absence of light. That is why the tiniest light destroys darkness. A little "something" is infinitely more than nothing. The more dark a place is, the more powerful a tiny light becomes to illuminate it!

God is the light of man (John 1). God made everyone to live forever in His presence, or the power source of life. God is the ONLY true power source, nothing can exist apart from His will for it to exist. He created ALL things and by His will they exist. Nothing that was made can exist apart from Him (Colossians 1:13-20). BUT, this is the crux of the problem the earth faces! God made certain things to dwell with Him in love! Specifically, God made people and angels to love Him. So, in order for love to be real, God had to give people and angels free will, so they could choose to love God back.

Tribulation is Caused by Love!

No free will = no love. But free will is risky! Not everyone wants to be with God forever. One-third of the angels chose evil, or the absence of God's perfect leadership of light. One-third of the angels created to live in perfect light chose darkness! Many people, at the prompting of Satan, the first one to rebel against the light, also choose to try to live apart from God, the power source of life.

Because God chose love, EVERYONE will get what they really desire in the end. God gets what He wants, which is a creation that lasts forever and also "lives" in love, and people either get life in the presence of that love, or the absence of life eternal, while still "lasting" forever.

God calls this awful condition of lasting forever apart from the source of life a "lake of fire", which is the experience of consumption and decay that never ends:

Revelation 20:15 And anyone not found written in the Book of Life was cast into the lake of fire.

So, this is the main purpose of the New Song: to demonstrate to all the earth what a wholehearted connection with the author of life really looks like. In one last generation, God will demonstrate to all of creation that wholeheartedly...with all of your time, money, emotion, and faith...making Him your strength is what will sustain people forever. He does this by making the consequences for this choice manifest on earth over a period of seven years, called the tribulation.

The point of this plan to release tribulation is very simple: God uses the least intense means necessary to reach the greatest number of people, at the deepest heart level, without ever violating their free will (I steal this phrasing from Mike Bickle. It is more simple and powerful than any other I know of).

God refuses to violate free will, because He refuses to violate love. BUT, He is a good Father who also refuses to sit idly by and watch His beloved creation elect to exist forever in a state of death. The cost of sin IS death. That will never change. So God will "turn up the heat" in sevenfold (perfect) increases three (complete) times. This is described in the Book of Revelation as seals, trumpets and bowls. These are all intended to convince the last generation to choose to live in the light of man before that choice is made permanent.

Sin is the choice for the absence of God and His leadership, and the consequence, or the cost, of that choice is darkness, which is the absence of the source of life. This is what the tree of the knowledge of good and evil was all about!

Adam and Eve were created with the introductory knowledge of good. God is good, and every good thing flows out of His very being. He is an infinite well of goodness and beauty, and every good and perfect thing flows from Him continually:

James 1:17 Every good gift and every perfect gift is from above, and comes down from the Father of lights, with whom there is no variation or shadow of turning.

Adam and Eve walked and talked with God face to face. The knowledge of GOOD was fully available to them at the time of creation, if they would simply stay in the process of talking with, listening to, and believing Him! God never intended to withhold all knowledge from them, but wanted to be a dad and lead them, over time, into the fullness of knowledge. However, God did not force Adam and Eve to stay in the relationship of loving who He was as a Father.

The one choice for free will, or the choice to say "no" to perfect love was the tree of the knowledge of good AND evil. This was the choice to contrast that knowledge of good with the knowledge of the absence of good.

The choice to eat from the tree was the same as saying "let's find out what life apart from God looks like." This is the same as saying "thanks, but no thanks" to life in the fullness of God's unending light and love.

Adam and Eve didn't want God's absence, but they wanted what they thought was "more" than God had given them, which was the knowledge of life apart from Him. This was actually "less" than God had given them, because they desired the knowledge of what life would be like in less light...which is evil, the absence of God.

Lukewarm = Loss of Life

The fall of man was really a choice for a "half-hearted" relationship with the infinite source of life. Adam and Eve were tricked into less by a promise of a fuller life outside of wholehearted narrow desire for God. If only God was our only investment strategy, our only entertainment strategy, our only family counsel, our dream of success, our long-missing love... If only God was actually our only desire that every other desire had to pass through. If only God was a seal on our hearts and on our arms. How different we would be.

Options are literally killing us, yet we wonder why we are dull, and spiritually bored, and our kids don't care about God, and our cities dive deeper and deeper into corruption, greed, and murder. So many options for more simply give us less and less. The lie that caused the fall of man, literally the same lie we claim to have been freed of when we "got saved," literally kills us every day. The same lie Adam and Eve fell for is being foisted on the Church of our day...in our churches..in our homes and hearts. Limiting the options, fasting and praying, is the only way out of this Venus fly trap of "western success."

We get more by narrowing our focus on the actual source of satisfaction. Mankind was created with a perfect, infinite, capacity to dwell in the presence of an infinite God who made us to be fully satisfied forever. Adam and Eve were infinite in their capacity to encounter God's infinite brightness. When they chose to agree with the knowledge of life away from God, they chose some measure of darkness. Suddenly, by choosing to take in some measure of darkness, there was a limit to the amount of light Adam and Eve could experience. Anything less than infinite, is "infinitely less", and suddenly God's infinite bright glory became deadly to them, the same way a flashlight is deadly to darkness. The cost of sin IS death.

Half-heartedness is a serious problem!! Half-heartedness is what introduced death to God's infinite creation. Trying to connect part of your life to God, while still attempting to remain at "arms length" from His leadership is the most dangerous proposition.

Obeying God is coming under His leadership, letting Him be the Father again and humbling ourselves back to the position of kids listening for further instruction. The law was given to Moses to show mankind what that looks like. The law will never change. What God calls good is good forever. Many modern Christians don't understand this, and think they can have God's presence without His leadership. Because of love, because of free will, God has always allowed this "less than full" relationship with Himself. Everyone gets what they want, and many have attempted a half-hearted relationship with God, some even successfully, and they will forever be "least" in God's kingdom:

Matthew 5:18-19 For assuredly, I say to you, till heaven and earth pass away, one jot or one tittle will by no means pass from the law till all is fulfilled. Whoever therefore breaks one of the least of these commandments, and teaches men so, shall be called least in the kingdom of heaven; but whoever does and teaches them, he shall be called great in the kingdom of heaven.

At the return of Jesus, there will be "great" and "small" people in the kingdom. They will all have the same legal position, but their living condition will be vastly different. Just like there are many citizens in the USA, but they don't all share the same living condition:

Revelation 19:5 Then a voice came from the throne, saying, "Praise our God, all you His servants and those who fear Him, both small and great!"

The option to be lukewarm and still in a relationship with Jesus will continue to be an option until the day Jesus splits the sky. But, this choice will be harder and harder to live in. The events Jesus will allow to touch the Church are designed to move us from lukewarm into red-hot. The longer the Church tries to stay balanced, the more painful the events will seem to her.

The Bible vividly describes God "turning up the heat" in one generation to force everyone into a choice: Love Him wholeheartedly and find safety in His presence NOW...or approach Him casually and "fall away." This is called the "valley of decision" in the Book of Joel:

Joel 3:14 Multitudes, multitudes in the valley of decision! For the day of the Lord (His second coming) *is near in the valley of decision.*

Many are unprepared for this. Half-hearted, "lukewarm," Jesus followers are actually the most common kind in the mostly un-persecuted western Church. Luke warm believers are people who have their legal position set, meaning they are actually in the Church, but they measure their life, and thus desire to build their comfort and security, in the world. Jesus is entirely against this living condition:

Revelation 3:15-17 "I know your works, that you are neither cold nor hot. I could wish you were cold or hot. So then, because you are lukewarm, and neither cold nor hot, I will vomit you out of My mouth. Because you say, 'I am rich, have become wealthy, and have need of nothing'—and do not know that you are wretched, miserable, poor, blind, and naked—

The release of the New Song, or David's Tabernacle, is the context which Jesus will use to draw out and express wholeheartedness. You have to be wholehearted in your love for, and faith in, God to make your primary plan to weather the worst trouble to ever hit planet earth "to sing and pray to Jesus." Right now, many are getting more and more alarmed by the events happening in the earth. Singing and praying, which is making God your strength, as your solution to problems and your plan to get satisfied is a risky choice to make, but it is what God will use to demonstrate a difference between His people and those bound for a lake of fire:

Psalms 37:5-6 Commit your way to the Lord , Trust also in Him, And He shall bring it to pass. He shall bring forth your righteousness as the light...

Only One Thing Will Really Work

David's Tabernacle raised up globally IS Jesus' plan for His Bride in the last generation, specifically in the last 7 years leading up to Jesus' return. This will be a unique time of trouble intended to convince the world to repent and agree with God. God desires no one would perish, but that all would come into agreement with His leadership and live in His light forever, just what He said was "very good" in Genesis 1:31:

II Peter 3:9 The Lord is not slack concerning His promise, as some count slackness, but is longsuffering toward us, not willing that any should perish but that all should come to repentance.

So this is the plan of God: allow a time of trouble in which the dark gets darkest and the light gets brightest, so all will choose what they really want. This is what Jesus clearly described His return looking like. This is the essence of the parable of the wheat and the tares: sin and wickedness will mature (you can see this accelerating right before your eyes) in geographic locations that agree with it, and righteousness (the wheat) will mature (this also is happening right before our eyes) in geographic locations that agree with righteousness. God really honors the choices of geographic locations. Think of Nineveh, Sodom, or Egypt. Wherever there is a geographic location that agrees with evil, judgment IS coming. Wherever there is agreement with God's leadership, even right smack dab in the middle of darkness, God will save and protect those people agreeing with Him. In the midst of the judgment of Pharaoh, God protected the people of Moses:

Exodus 8:22 But this time I will spare the region of Goshen, where my people live. No flies will be found there. Then you will know that I am the Lord and that I am present even in the heart of your land.

Lot had to be taken out of Sodom before the angels could destroy the city. To look back, as Lot's wife did, was to desire some of what Sodom had, this is the same as agreeing with its "fruit" of desiring life apart from God's leadership. If you desire what a place under judgment desires, you will share in its same fate. God ALWAYS honors desire, because He has committed to free will. God has committed to free will because He has committed to love.

This is the judgment pattern seen throughout the Bible: the righteous separated, the geographic location of refuge established by those wholeheartedly agreeing with God, and everyone who is willing to respond and desire God's leadership flourishes in a promised land. If you look back (desire what those under judgment desire) you share in their fate:

Genesis 19:15, 17, 20, 22-26 When the morning dawned, the angels urged Lot to hurry, saying, "Arise, take your wife and your two daughters who are here, lest you be consumed in the punishment of the city."...

So it came to pass, when they had brought them outside, that he said, "Escape for your life! Do not look behind you nor stay anywhere in the plain. Escape to the mountains, lest you be destroyed."...

But Lot didn't want to go to the mountains. He selected a different geographic location:

See now, this city is near enough to flee to, and it is a little one; please let me escape there (is it not a little one?) and my soul shall live." ...

The angel agreed and told Lot what is true every time God judges a place "God refuses to let the righteous share in the judgment of the wicked":

Hurry, escape there. For I cannot do anything until you arrive there..."

...The sun had risen upon the earth when Lot entered Zoar. Then the Lord rained brimstone and fire on Sodom and Gomorrah, from the Lord out of the heavens. So He overthrew those cities, all the plain, all the inhabitants of the cities, and what grew on the ground. But his wife looked back behind him, and she became a pillar of salt.

Lot's wife regretted leaving wicked Sodom, where her children had been abused, and the people of the city were awfully wicked! She agreed with some part of what Sodom had to offer enough to look back with regret for being saved from it. This desire for evil cost her. When God offers an escape, He expects wholehearted agreement with it.

Look at the Exodus: the sea split, the pillar of fire, all the plagues that touched Egypt and not Goshen, where Israel dwelled right in the middle! But that generation was not wholehearted in trusting the supernatural God:

Exodus 16:3 And the children of Israel said to them, "Oh, that we had died by the hand of the Lord in the land of Egypt, when we sat by the pots of meat and when we ate bread to the full! For you have brought us out into this wilderness to kill this whole assembly with hunger."

This is what God said about this half-hearted generation:

Psalms 95:10-11 For forty years I was grieved with that generation, And said, 'It is a people who go astray in their hearts, And they do not know My ways.' So I swore in My wrath, 'They shall not enter My rest.' "

The global building of the Tabernacle of David, called the New Song, is Jesus' plan for rescue BECAUSE it requires wholehearted commitment to God as our strength. The intensity that is coming requires everyone to choose their strength: man's plan or invisible Jesus (Joel 3:14). We make God our strength by actually expressing our trust in Him to save us. This will be expressed by night and day talking to Him through music, just like David's generation did.

The entire earth will be judged, or sifted. God will use the intensity of the events to shake geographic locations until everything that can be shaken has been shaken. Just like the shaking of a sieve causes everything too small to pass through, the seals, trumpets, and bowls will shake out everyone who doesn't really want God all the way. If God is your entire plan, your entire plan will not be shaken!:

Amos 9:9-12 "For I will give the command and will shake Israel along with the other nations (global shaking) *as grain is shaken in a sieve, yet not one true kernel will be lost. But all the sinners will die by the sword— all those who say, 'Nothing bad will happen to us.'*(requires "being ready" seeing the trouble coming and preparing) *"In that day I will restore the fallen house of David. I will repair its damaged walls. From the ruins I will rebuild it and restore its former glory.* (This is to provide cities of habitation to protect those agreeing with God's leadership enough to actually spend the time and effort building 24-hour prayer) *And Israel will possess what is left of Edom and all the nations I have called to be mine*. (This Tabernacle building will be global...Israel and every nation Jesus will own) *The Lord has spoken, and he will do these things.*

The judgment and the rescue released by the New Song go hand in hand, by design, in order to let the earth see the difference .

Isaiah 24:1-3, 13-16 Look! The Lord is about to destroy the earth and make it a vast wasteland. He devastates the surface of the earth and scatters the people. Priests and laypeople, servants and masters, maids and mistresses, buyers and sellers, lenders and borrowers, bankers and debtors—none will be spared. The earth will be completely emptied and looted.... The Lord has spoken! Throughout the earth the story is the same— only a remnant is left, like the stray olives left on the tree or the few grapes left on the vine after harvest. But all who are left shout and sing for joy (New Song!). *Those in the west praise the Lord 's majesty. In eastern lands, give glory to the Lord. In the lands beyond the sea, praise the name of the Lord , the God of Israel. We hear songs of praise from the ends of the earth, songs that give glory to the Righteous One! But my heart is heavy with grief. Weep for me, for I wither away. Deceit still prevails, and treachery is everywhere.*

The New Song is the plan to make a difference that is visible between the wheat and the tares. As the Bride draws together in geographic locations and does the hard work of coming out of the world and committing to night and day prayer, increasingly she will agree with Jesus about judging the evil world system she is "coming out of." If the Bride turns back, if she tries to keep one foot in the world and one foot in Jesus' leadership, she will run the huge risk of falling away. The New Song REQUIRES a wholehearted, all-in, commitment, by design. This will sift the wheat, the true grains, and it will purify and de-spot the Bride. Not because God's has forced her into anything, but by the Bride's own desire. Everyone gets what they want in the end!

The events are so intense though, that MANY will fall away. The cost of agreeing with God is everything. If you look back, if you approach Him and His desired location of safety any less than wholeheartedly, it will cost you. That is why Jesus warned the 7 churches before the trouble to "overcome."

There WILL BE a great falling away. This means many will quit following Jesus. The New Testament declares this over and over. This is what Jesus is warning the Church in Revelation 2 and 3 about: the time of trouble coming, and those who are not ready, who don't prepare in advance, will not overcome the trouble that starts in Revelation 6. All of the issues identified by Jesus as needing to be addressed by the seven churches of Revelation 2 and 3 are answered fully in the Sermon on the Mount. The Sermon on the Mount is the formula for dwelling with others in right relationships, and making God your strength rather than money, earthly status, or comfort.

The Tabernacle of David, or the New Song, IS Jesus' plan because the only way it is sustainable is through wholehearted loyalty to Jesus expressed in obedience as described in the Sermon on the Mount. What I mean is, the only way a group of people can get along in the costly process of building night and day prayer is through the principals laid out in the Sermon on the Mount. If Jesus is going to get a pure and spotless Bride, then the Tabernacle of David is the washing machine that will agitate, rinse, and soap up that very Bride!

God WILL have a pure and spotless Bride for His son, and she will get cleaned up in trying to build 24-hour prayer with others loyal to Jesus. Unity comes from sharing a common experience of dying to ourselves, because of our great desire to agree with Jesus, not from agreeing about minor points of doctrine, while putting aside major points, or worse yet, throwing out doctrine all together. Commitment at cost is the bond of unity. It is committing to be more like Jesus by asking for it that produces unity in agreement with the Bible.

The New Song will undo thousands of years of division, because the only way it is sustainable is by dwelling together in shared commitment to keep the "fire on the altar." THIS is what will unite a Bride growing in love and obedience, all the while seeing a growing faith transform the land they dwell in!

Psalms 33:2-4, 11, 17-20 Praise the Lord with the harp; Make melody to Him with an instrument of ten strings. Sing to Him a New Song; Play skillfully with a shout of joy. For the word of the Lord is right, And all His work is done in truth....

... The counsel of the Lord stands forever, The plans of His heart to all generations....

... A horse is a vain hope for safety; Neither shall it deliver any by its great strength. Behold, the eye of the Lord is on those who fear Him, On those who hope in His mercy, To deliver their soul from death, And to keep them alive in famine. Our soul waits for the Lord ; He is our help and our shield.

Unity is the Point of the New Song
Again, the phrase "New Song" refers to the end-time prayer to music (worship) movement promised to be "raised up" by God in the generation the Lord will return to. God is ACTUALLY doing this right now. Thousands of geographic locations all over the globe are operating in some level of night and day prayer with a vision of it related to the return of Jesus. Amos said that it is through the night and day prayer movement that those loyal to God...true kernels of grain...would be kept through the time of shaking (Amos 9:10-11).

Joel (chapter 2) said that coming together as a community of believers, praying in one accord, would transform the land, give God a location to pour His Spirit upon in signs and wonders, and equip His people to fulfill the great commission with power, so that "everyone who calls on the name of the Lord will be saved."

The New Song will REQUIRE the Bride to die to herself and come together in unity to keep the fire on the altar. This brilliant plan is the context Jesus will use in a time of trouble to get what He prayed for in John 17:

John 17:20-21 "I do not pray for these alone, but also for those who will believe in Me through their word; that they all may be one, as You, Father, are in Me, and I in You; that they also may be one in Us, that the world may believe that You sent Me.

This will happen as the trouble increases, and the Bride gathers to seek the Lord as her solution. The "close quarters" and "hard work" of keeping the diverse streams of the Bride on the same page will require an all-in commitment to Jesus (sharing in His death to self), which will produce true unity. Unity doesn't happen when we all agree with each other about Jesus. Unity happens when we agree with Jesus about each other! True unity keeps Jesus in the center, and makes what He says is true MORE visible. True unity doesn't hide Jesus, it unveils Him more to the earth.

And unity is what we will need in order to build, and keep, 24-hour prayer to music going in a time of trouble! As we all lock our gaze on Jesus and begin running toward Him with our whole hearts, the trajectory of our paths will naturally draw us closed to each other. Picture the spokes of a wheel, which are closer at the hub than way out at the tire. If Jesus is the center, as we all run toward Him, we must get closer together! Jesus is going to shake everything that can be shaken, and there is only one place that cannot be shaken: WHERE HE STANDS! Jesus prayed in John 17 that we would be "one" with each other and Him, so we will stand right where He is. The night and day praying Bride will produce geographic locations that will not be shaken, but she will do more than that, she will agree with Jesus about the "shaking" itself in her geographic place of intercession and release the judgments along with Jesus!

This is God's design for operating in the earth: He looks for a man or woman to agree with Him.

Ezekiel 22:30 So I sought for a man among them who would make a wall, and stand in the gap before Me on behalf of the land, that I

should not destroy it; but I found no one.

God has committed to partnering with people to carry out His plans on earth. This is because He has given leadership of the earth to mankind. When God gives something, He REALLY gives it. This is why prayer is necessary. Many wonder why God wants us to pray if He already knows everything! It is because the verbal agreement of mankind on earth is necessary, based on God's sovereign decision to give dominion of the earth to mankind.

Genesis 1:28 Then God blessed them, and God said to them, "Be fruitful and multiply; fill the earth and subdue it; have dominion over the fish of the sea, over the birds of the air, and over every living thing that moves on the earth."

Psalms 115:16 The heaven, even the heavens, are the Lord 's; But the earth He has given to the children of men.

If my dad came to my house and wanted to see something changed, He would ask me to agree! I remember being a young man and needing to re-do the roof of my house. My dad knew how to do it. Without His help it wasn't going to happen, but I didn't sit on the couch while he re-did the roof. I went up on the roof and agreed with him in the work. In the process we got closer, the roof got done, and the house was made better.

This is a simple picture of what God desires: His family agreeing with Him about the cultivating of the most amazing Garden by speaking and agreeing on things that He actually does by the power of the Spirit! This is how creation worked: the Father had the plan, Jesus spoke the words, and the Spirit did the stuff!

This is how Jesus modeled life for His disciples. When Jesus sent out His disciples in Luke 9, He basically told them "take nothing with you but your desire and your mouth and go change the world by speaking words and seeing the Spirit agree with your words in the release of power"

Mark 6:7-8, 12-13 And He called the twelve to Himself, and began to send them out two by two, and gave them power over unclean spirits.

*He commanded them to take nothing for the journey except a staff—
no bag, no bread, no copper in their money belts— So they went out
and preached that people should repent. And they cast out many
demons, and anointed with oil many who were sick, and healed them.*

This was the first picture of the great commission. Why the
staff, Jesus? Where you afraid they were going to trip?!! No! They took
their staffs as a sign of what Jesus would do in the final fulfilling of the
great commission! The final disciples are going to lead the whole earth
out of the end-time Pharaoh's camp into the promised land through
judgments, signs and wonders! Moses had a staff he used to release the
judgments and split the sea. Jesus' disciples are going to fill the role of
the end-time Moses! God looks for people to agree with Him about
what needs doing in the earth, and the end-time Bride is going to be
rocking out prayers to song that will release the judgments! Just like
Moses held out His staff!

*Exodus 4:16-17 Aaron will be your spokesman to the people. He will be
your mouthpiece, and you will stand in the place of God for him, telling
him what to say. And take your shepherd's staff with you, and use it to
perform the miraculous signs I have shown you."*

On the way to Egypt to command Pharaoh to release God's
people, God gave Moses a sign that this whole event was simply a
smaller picture pointing to something way bigger than Egypt. This was
pointing to the way Jesus would get His family back, called in the Bible a
"great harvest!"

*Exodus 4:24-26 On the way to Egypt, at a place where Moses and his
family had stopped for the night, the Lord confronted him and was
about to kill him. But Moses' wife, Zipporah, took a flint knife and
circumcised her son. She touched his feet with the foreskin and said,
"Now you are a bridegroom of blood to me."* (When she said "a
bridegroom of blood," she was referring to the circumcision.) *After that,
the Lord left him alone.*

The New Song Will Judge Every Other Plan

The end-time Bride will partner with the Jesus, the groom, and through the words spoken in the authority of the Bride washed in the Blood, will release the very power of God in unity as the faithful witness that Her Groom is behind all that is happening in the earth. This will be incredibly disruptive. Mankind will call God evil for letting the intensity increase, but the Bride will say "no! His judgments are His love!" Even the worst judgments are better than the choice made permanent to try to live a life apart from the author of life, which is a lake of fire forever, where the worm never dies and the fire never goes out.

Jesus' plan, written out in the Book of Revelation, is to use the least intense means necessary, to reach the greatest number of people, at the deepest heart level, without ever violating free will. The intensity is designed to save people. The Bride will declare this to the world as the end-time "Moses." The events are numbered and ordered. 3 always comes after 2! and the Bride will know exactly what to sing for next. We' ll be singing and saying: "Come Lord, release the next trumpet! We long for Eden, and to be with you. Your judgments are Your love! Shake the world so they might choose you. We'll tell them why you are doing it!"

Romans 10:14-15 How then shall they call on Him in whom they have not believed? And how shall they believe in Him of whom they have not heard? And how shall they hear without a preacher? And how shall they preach unless they are sent? As it is written: "How beautiful are the feet of those who preach the gospel of peace, Who bring glad tidings of good things!"

In the passage above, Paul was quoting Isaiah 52:7, which was immediately followed with a description of the "sent" ones:

Isaiah 52:8 Your watchmen shall lift up their voices, With their voices they shall sing together; For they shall see eye to eye When the Lord brings back Zion.

This is a major point of the New Song: uniting with Jesus to release judgment that will SAVE people by causing them to repent before it is too late. The prayers of the singing Bride release the judgments:

Revelation 8:4-6 And the smoke of the incense, with the prayers of the saints, ascended before God from the angel's hand. Then the angel took the censer, filled it with fire from the altar, and threw it to the earth. And there were noises, thunderings, lightnings, and an earthquake. So the seven angels who had the seven trumpets prepared themselves to sound.

Revelation 15:2-4 And I saw something like a sea of glass mingled with fire, and those who have the victory over the beast, over his image and over his mark and over the number of his name, standing on the sea of glass, having harps of God. They sing the song of Moses, the servant of God, and the song of the Lamb, saying: "Great and marvelous are Your works, Lord God Al...mighty! Just and true are Your ways, O King of the saints! Who shall not fear You, O Lord, and glorify Your name? For You alone are holy. For all nations shall come and worship before You, For Your judgments have been manifested."

Standing on the sea of glass in this scene in Revelation 15 are all of the saints from Adam to today. At the sounding of the 7th trumpet, the "mystery of God" is complete:

Revelation 10:7 but in the days of the sounding of the seventh angel, when he is about to sound, the mystery of God would be finished, as He declared to His servants the prophets.

Revelation 11:15 Then the seventh angel sounded: And there were loud voices in heaven, saying, "The kingdoms of this world have become the kingdoms of our Lord and of His Christ, and He shall reign forever and ever!"

This is the last trumpet. What is the mystery of God? It is the rapture, which is the gathering together of the Bride on the sea of glass, and for the first time we will be eye to eye with the Groom. This is the "walking down the aisle" of the Bride. It is the beginning of the physical marriage, which is the face-to-face the union of the Firstborn to His Bride. Jesus will freely share His inheritance bought with His perfect sacrifice with anyone who would say "yes" to His love, THAT is the mystery of God!   It is the wedding of the Lamb, which starts at the rapture!:

I Corinthians 2:7-9 But we speak the wisdom of God in a mystery, the hidden wisdom which God ordained before the ages for our glory, which none of the rulers of this age knew; for had they known, they would not have crucified the Lord of glory. But as it is written: "Eye has not seen, nor ear heard, Nor have entered into the heart of man The things which God has prepared for those who love Him."

I Corinthians 15:51-52 Behold, I tell you a mystery: We shall not all sleep, but we shall all be changed— in a moment, in the twinkling of an eye, at the last trumpet. For the trumpet will sound, and the dead will be raised incorruptible, and we shall be changed.

Ephesians 5:31-32 "For this reason a man shall leave his father and mother and be joined to his wife, and the two shall become one flesh." This is a great mystery, but I speak concerning Christ and the church.

Revelation is Rooted in Exodus
The song of the wedding is what the Bride is singing on the sea of glass, which is the song of Moses. The pure and spotless Bride of the last generation, the third transitional generation, along with all those who passed into heaven before her, will stand together with the Groom and sing the song of the first transitional generation, the song they sang as they supernaturally crossed the Red Sea on dry ground! Can you imagine being in the same company as Moses singing the song of His generation!

To understand the Revelation of Jesus Christ, it is ESSENTIAL to understand Exodus. The same elements of the Exodus from Egypt will be present throughout the events of Revelation! These are intentionally connected to the Exodus so that we might understand Revelation. Unfortunately, modern teaching of Revelation rarely connects it to Exodus. This is error which results in myths being fabricated to explain away the intensity. If you know anything about the Exodus story, you know the intensity was real and quite intentional. God used the intensity to reveal to Pharaoh that agreement with God was wise. Many of the plagues of Egypt will be intentionally repeated in the trumpet and bowl judgments described in Revelation 16!

Here are some facets to the Exodus story that are essential for the Bride to understand. The end time 24 hour prayer to music movement:

1. The plagues in Egypt, where those in rebellion to God lived, did not affect Goshen, where God's people lived. The Israelites had to take some steps in agreement with God (the Passover), but God was using the plagues to bring agreement. If you are already in agreement with God, you don't "need" correction. God is a good and precise Father, not a sloppy painter carelessly releasing dangerous things on the land. We agree with Him now in building the "Tabernacle of David" in our lands, and He will make a difference between those places that agree with Him and the locations that ignore His formula to weather this generation:

Exodus 8:22-23 And in that day I will set apart the land of Goshen, in which My people dwell, that no swarms of flies shall be there, in order that you may know that I am the Lord in the midst of the land. I will make a difference between My people and your people. Tomorrow this sign shall be." ' "

2. God's plagues on Egypt grew progressively worse, and were a well-designed and thought-out plan to use the least intense means necessary to reach the Egyptians to agree with God without violating their free will. As Pharaoh resisted and chose to harden his heart, God helped him get what he chose: a hard heart. Everyone gets what they want in the end, including God. God gave the entire plan to Moses before he ever went before Pharaoh:

Exodus 4:28-31 So Moses told Aaron all the words of the Lord who had sent him, and all the signs which He had commanded him. Then Moses and Aaron went and gathered together all the elders of the children of Israel. And Aaron spoke all the words which the Lord had spoken to Moses. Then he did the signs in the sight of the people. So the people believed; and when they heard that the Lord had visited the children of Israel and that He had looked on their affliction, then they bowed their

heads and worshiped.

The Israelites didn't fear God's plan to bring judgment in the land they lived! They celebrated the plan as a sign that God knew their plight!

If you look at the Revelation judgments as negative for you, you need to begin a conversation with God about that because you are either unclear about a.) God's power to protect you, or b.) God's desire to protect you. The Israelites saw the judgments as a good thing, and we are supposed to, as well!

3. God didn't release judgment directly, but instead used Aaron and Moses, the people of Israel, to release them. This is a Biblical principal that is woven into creation. God uses people to accomplish His plans for the earth. He refuses to violate this principle, because to do so would violate His command that man would have dominion over the earth. When God wants to do something on the earth, He looks for a person to agree with Him.

The Bride Will Be The Witness of Jesus on Earth
The worshiping/praying Bride is the end-time Moses and Aaron who will release the judgments in agreement with Jesus until He returns and sets up His kingdom on earth as the Man Christ Jesus. This is the clear story of the Book of Revelation. As the Bride matures, she will walk in greater measures of authority.

Two people, true leaders of the Bride, will release the judgments of God at will from the center of Jerusalem. These two end-time prophets, members of the end-time worshiping Bride, will protect the geographic locations of the Bride as the enemy forces try to attack the towns of the Bride. Right in the heart of antichrist's home base, these two natural-bodied people will speak and release the judgments geographically to protect the night and day worshiping Bride!:

Revelation 11:3-6 And I will give power to my two witnesses, and they will prophesy one thousand two hundred and sixty days, clothed in sackcloth." These are the two olive trees and the two lampstands standing before the God of the earth. And if anyone wants to harm them, fire proceeds from their mouth and devours their enemies. And if anyone wants to harm them, he must be killed in this manner. These have power to shut heaven, so that no rain falls in the days of their prophecy; and they have power over waters to turn them to blood, and to strike the earth with all plagues, as often as they desire.

The two witnesses of Jesus are the pinnacle of a reality the whole Bride will share in. The Bride is going to walk in increasing measures of authority as she agrees with each other and Jesus more and more. That is the point of the Book of Revelation! Jesus is looking for a Bride who, when the world looks at her, they see Jesus! Just as He said "when you have seen me, you have seen the Father," Jesus is going to have a Bride who can say "if you have seen me, you have seen my Groom!" This begins as we agree with Jesus that His judgments ARE His love!

John 17:20-23 "I do not pray for these alone, but also for those who will believe in Me through their word; that they all may be one, as You, Father, are in Me, and I in You; that they also may be one in Us, that the world may believe that You sent Me. And the glory which You gave Me I have given them, that they may be one just as We are one: I in them, and You in Me; that they may be made perfect in one, and that the world may know that You have sent Me, and have loved them as You have loved Me.

Revelation 14:1-5 Then I looked, and behold, a Lamb standing on Mount Zion, and with Him one hundred and forty-four thousand, having His Father's name written on their foreheads. And I heard a voice from heaven, like the voice of many waters, and like the voice of loud thunder. And I heard the sound of harpists playing their harps. They sang as it were a New Song before the throne, before the four living creatures, and the elders; and no one could learn that song except the hundred and forty-four thousand who were redeemed from the earth. These are the ones who were not defiled with women, for they are virgins. These are the ones who follow the Lamb wherever He goes. These were redeemed from among men, being firstfruits to God and to the Lamb. And in their mouth was found no deceit, for they are without fault before the throne of God.

The "New Song" is the context God will use to "extract" purity and spotlessness from His Bride. This happens in full before Jesus returns. God has a brilliant process that requires a "time of great trouble" to touch the earth in order to get all people in one generation to choose whether they trust in invisible Jesus or the "work of their own hands," a man based plan dreamt up by the ultimate man, the antichrist.

Everyone who chooses man's strength will bear the mark of the man, called the mark of the beast. Everyone who chooses invisible Jesus will be marked by His presence, which will be the Spirit POURED OUT on all flesh. Investing your trust to God through prayer in a time of trouble instead of agreeing with the rest of the world about a man's "action plan" to make the earth peaceful, just, and good, will mature into the New Song.

Everyone who makes this "crazy" choice to make their lives about expressing desire to Jesus and seeing Him answer in power will get what they want! Everyone who chooses to trust in unreliable self-centered man will get what they want, too. This is the promised end time "valley of decision":

Joel 3:14-16 Multitudes, multitudes in the valley of decision! For the day of the LORD is near in the valley of decision. (15) The sun and moon will grow dark, And the stars will diminish their brightness. (16) The LORD also will roar from Zion, And utter His voice from Jerusalem; The heavens and earth will shake; But the LORD will be a shelter for His people, And the strength of the children of Israel.

The Safety in Singing NOW
Right now, God is gathering His Church in geographic locations to sing and pray night and day, as we express the desire of our final choice. This subject is so vast in the Bible I could never capture it in one writing, but the idea is this: the night and day expression of desire for God to be the answer will result in "safe zones" created in before the time of trouble. These safe zones will be transformed into supernaturally active areas where the Holy Spirit begins releasing miraculous signs and people begin relationships with Jesus en mass, thousands and even tens of thousands at a time. Then, as the differences between these locations and the locations that don't do

this, become more obvious, people who want to "call on the name of the Lord to be saved" will migrate from the "desolate areas" into these safe zones. Crazy? A little. Biblical? Totally. Happening right now? Yes.

As communities of people try to build night and day prayer, they quickly find out it is COSTLY. It is impossible to do this half-heartedly. Yes, you can ride on someone else's wholeheartedness for a while, BUT if you aren't growing in your own wholeheartedness while in a core group of wholehearted people spending their strength on making God the strength of the community, it will not work. This is God's design. He ONLY loves wholeheartedly, and is looking for a people that will wholeheartedly love Him back. He wants to be "equally yoked" in the relationship. These wholehearted ones are the ones who will lead many to righteousness and will "shine like the stars forever." They will have high places of authority in the new physical real government coming to planet earth:

Daniel 12:1-3 "At that time Michael shall stand up, The great prince who stands watch over the sons of your people; And there shall be a time of trouble, Such as never was since there was a nation, Even to that time. And at that time your people shall be delivered, Every one who is found written in the book. And many of those who sleep in the dust of the earth shall awake, Some to everlasting life, Some to shame and everlasting contempt. Those who are wise shall shine Like the brightness of the firmament, And those who turn many to righteousness Like the stars forever and ever.

This is a radical lifestyle in the "secret place." This isn't about starting a new cult, or some new way to encounter God. The only way this whole "night and day prayer creating safe zones" thing works is if at home, by yourself, you are seeking the Lord with all your heart, mind, soul, and strength, and then you bring the fruit of that encounter into the place of corporate prayer. This is not new. This is the same way Christians were always supposed to live. Coming to Church gatherings to pour out, not be filled up.

Consumerism has not only watered down the American Church experience to a show, it has killed wholeheartedness in the homes across western culture. Church has become another activity on the schedule instead of the gathering place to pour out offerings of worship and prayer corporately that reflect vibrant encounters with God privately.   This is all about to change.

The trouble Jesus allows is going to force the change. The only church that will survive the Great Tribulation (the final 3.5 years of the seven year tribulation) is a pure and spotless Bride, by design. Communities that get ready in advance and start filling the lamps with the oil of encountering Jesus will be the ones that flourish through the trouble.

One of the "first fruits" of this is reflected in the kids of those who make the choice for wholehearted response to God in the approaching time of trouble. This is what the first part of Revelation 14 is all about. The 144,000 described in Revelation 14 are leaders of a promised generation where God is turning the hearts of the fathers to the kids and the kids to the fathers:

Malachi 4:5-6 Behold, I will send you Elijah the prophet Before the coming of the great and dreadful day of the LORD. (6) And he will turn The hearts of the fathers to the children, And the hearts of the children to their fathers, Lest I come and strike the earth with a curse.

This promised generation is one where kids are raised in a culture of purity. The parents that respond and build the New Song will come out (spiritually and physically) of a culture that values worldly desire, the kids will see the difference it makes, and the kids will see chasing after purity as totally worth it. Praying night and day? "Of course, that is what the Church does," they say. What was weird and uncomfortable for the parents, will be totally natural for their kids. "why wouldn't we pray all the time?" they will say. "When we pray God changes our whole city! Duh!"

Revelation 14 promises the kids of the New Song cities will be so enamored with God, and so excited that Jesus is about to return, that they will be, as a lifestyle, pressing in to Him and expressing their desire to Him in such a way that He answers with power. They will hear the voice of Jesus (many waters) and the Father (thunder) with CLARITY. And what do Jesus and the Father have to say? "Here are songs just for you that have chosen Me! Only you are authorized to sing them. These New Songs will bless the whole earth, but I will mark you with my presence."

Revelation 14:2 And I heard a voice from heaven, like the voice of many waters, and like the voice of loud thunder. And I heard the sound of harpists playing their harps. They sang as it were a NEW SONG before the throne, before the four living creatures, and the elders; and no one could learn that song except the hundred and forty-four thousand who were redeemed from the earth. These are the ones who were not defiled with women, for they are virgins. These are the ones who follow the Lamb wherever He goes. These were redeemed from among men, being firstfruits to God and to the Lamb. And in their mouth was found no deceit, for they are without fault before the throne of God.

The passage implies that this generation was recognized by their parents (spiritual and natural) who invested in them wholeheartedly, while they were young. To be undefiled in the most defiled culture to ever inhabit earth requires some INTENTION on the part of the older generation. Just like our sports culture raises up generations of new athletes that push the bar of performance, the Church, in areas where the older ones have a vision for it, will create a culture of intentionally, wholeheartedly, investing in kids that will push the envelope of purity. So much so that the kids will say, like Paul, "In this hour of history marriage is a distraction. I don't want anything to get in between me and the future God has for me." Paul foretold this heart attitude in relation to the end times:

1 Corinthians 7:29-33 But this I say, brethren, the time is short, so that from now on even those who have wives should be as though they had none, those who weep as though they did not weep, those who rejoice as though they did not rejoice, those who buy as though they did not possess, and those who use this world as not misusing it. For the form of this world is passing away. But I want you to be without care. He who is unmarried cares for the things of the Lord—how he may please the Lord. But he who is married cares about the things of the world— how he may please his wife.

Paul went on to say this wasn't for everyone, but that people that wanted to change the world in the time that was "short" would live this way. Any community can begin to invest in their kids in a way that will produce this heart attitude. The Bible promises a generation not "kept from marriage", but voluntarily choosing to forgo distractions, as they see the approaching and glorious King of kings actually respond to their wholehearted zeal. They will be so fascinated by Jesus they will "follow Him wherever He goes."

In the midst of the darkest hour of earth's history, communities of people that choose the hard work building of the night and day prayer movement will see a generation of young ones who wholeheartedly chase Jesus NATURALLY, because they watched and were convinced by their parents actual choices that demonstrated "He is worth it!"

Revelation: The Story of a Wedding- 5

He knows the heart of man
Formed perfect for His plan
Though His enemy once stole
Through the Mystery all shall know
That things are not always as they seem

A wedding in His eye
A Bride is His delight
Though today she cannot see
A gift promised, hers will be
For a purpose far more grand than trinkets, wine, and glamour

For there is strength in the bond
Chosen and revealed in perfect strife
When fire is applied in His wise measure

His own image will be seen
In the Bride of this great King
The world she will amaze with His splendor

Some will glory in the truth
Others harden in their pride
As He dashes everything
That would usurp Earth's one true King

His Bride's fiery image shining
The world in error cries still pining
For the comfort once they tasted
Every lesser thing lays wasted

But the companion of the Man
Who holds redemption as His plan
Declares day and night
There is pleasure and true might
In agreeing with the King
Who is reclaiming everything
With a Word He had created!

The Book of Revelation is the greatest revelation of who Jesus is in the Bible. Revelation Chapter 1 has 30 descriptions of Jesus in just a few paragraphs. This is the foundation to understand the rest of the book. The entire book portrays Jesus primarily as the only one worthy to rule the earth. But, He is a Bridegroom, too! Revelation is MOSTLY the story of a wedding. It is the context Jesus gives His Bride to "get ready."

The Book of Revelation is, in its simplest explanation, a story of the most amazing wedding in all of human history. Marriage is a legal relationship invented by God. We got the idea of marriage from Him, not the other way around. God defines marriage as two people legally agreeing to be so closely united they become one:

Genesis 2:24 Therefore a man shall leave his father and mother and be joined to his wife, and they shall become one flesh.

Love is Voluntary

God is very serious about unity. Revelation is the process of Jesus' Bride, currently a divided Church, being transformed from a bunch of un-unified "factions", into one pure and spotless Bride. Most people sitting in pews right now think Jesus is going to wave His hand some day and "make us" unified. He NEVER does anything like that!!

As is worth repeating, Jesus is committed to love, which means He is FULLY committed to free will. He offers an invitation, and people who love Him respond. He has always operated this way. He commands the wind and the waves, but He woos the hearts of men. Revelation is really the wooing process of Jesus, giving His Bride the context to choose to "get ready for her own wedding".

The modern Church generally reads the judgments in the Book of Revelation and initially think they are "bad." But the book is titled

"The Revelation of Jesus Christ," not the revelation of Satan, or the antichrist! Jesus says the judgments reveal who He is, and who His "other half" is to the world.

God has designed the entire plan described in the Book of Revelation to redeem those who are rebelling against Him, as a context for His Bride to agree with Him as she prays with Him for the release of those judgments, and for Her to come into such agreement with Him that she actually carries the very authority of Jesus on earth BEFORE He comes.

When Jesus comes, as described in Revelation 19 and 20, Heaven declares: She Has Made Herself Ready!!

Revelation 19:7 Let us be glad and rejoice and give Him glory, for the marriage of the Lamb has come, and His wife has made herself ready."

Jesus doesn't wave His hand and she is spotless! No! He gives her the space to agree with Him to become spotless during the most intense time in human history. The Bride gets credit for "making herself ready" but the truth is, Jesus was the one who gave her the events He has planned in His Word. If we use the New Song is a washing machine analogy, then the events of tribulation are the motor agitating and power the actual washing process. This brilliant plan is designed to make the Bride ready. Even the preparation for the wedding is a partnership between Jesus and His Bride:

Ephesians 5:25-27 Husbands, love your wives, just as Christ also loved the church and gave Himself for her, that He might sanctify and cleanse her with the washing of water by the word, that He might present her to Himself a glorious church, not having spot or wrinkle or any such thing, but that she should be holy and without blemish.

Offense Produces the Falling Away
The events of Revelation are Jesus' engagement present to His Bride. Many look at the present Jesus has planned to give to His Bride and they wish Jesus would get them a different present! This is because they don't understand, or really trust, that their groom is perfectly powerful and perfectly loving. If these two things are true, then no object of His love should be afraid of anything He has planned! He is not

worried or afraid of the tribulation He has planned. He has a fire He really wants to kindle, because that fire refines His Bride as she is protected, carried, kept, and actually made to FLOURISH through it.

The events of Revelation are intended to separate the wheat (those loyal to Jesus and His plans) from the tares (everyone else):

Luke 12:49, 51 "I came to send fire on the earth, and how I wish it were already kindled! Do you suppose that I came to give peace on earth? I tell you, not at all, but rather division.

Jesus isn't afraid of this fire. We shouldn't be afraid of what it will do either. He wants His Bride in such agreement with Him that we become a faithful witness to anyone who will listen that He loves them and they can call on His name! He isn't going to rain down tribulation on a bunch of unsuspecting people who don't even believe He is good, without giving them some people to explain what is happening. He has never operated that way. Just ask Jonah!

I want to be careful how I look at Jesus' engagement present. The present is actually designed to make me ready for greatness forever in governmental partnership with Jesus. If I look at the tribulation as negative and hope to escape receiving it, I will not get the benefit of owning it and I will be much less ready for life in full when it begins as it has always intended to be: face to face with God.

Many who are casual about their future husband will be offended by HIS tribulation gift. Many will "fall away" when they begin to receive His engagement present: the Great Tribulation. Many are hoping their husband has a better present in mind. Something more comfortable. That is not at all what Jesus described when speaking privately to His disciples:

Matthew 24:9-13 "Then they will deliver you up to tribulation and kill you, and you will be hated by all nations for My name's sake. And then many will be offended, will betray one another, and will hate one another. Then many false prophets will rise up and deceive many. And because lawlessness will abound, the love of many will grow cold. But he who endures to the end shall be saved.

Paul said this offense, or falling away, MUST happen before Jesus comes. Jesus is going to separate those loyal to Him, in the context of His engagement present, as part of the context He gives the Bride to make herself ready:

II Thessalonians 2:3 Let no one deceive you by any means; for that Day will not come unless the falling away comes first, and the man of sin is revealed, the son of perdition,

The Process of Purity

The Book of Revelation opens up with the first three chapters setting the stage for the wedding. Chapter one is all about the Groom. Chapters 2 and 3 are all about His immature Bride-to-be. She is kind of a sloppy mess, broken up into seven very different characteristic churches. Once the tribulation starts, those seven churches are never mentioned again, only the one Bride. The Bride becomes one, and spotless, THROUGH the tribulation. The Book of Revelation describes the process God uses to answer one of Jesus' last prayers before going to the cross:

John 17:20-26 "I do not pray for these alone, but also for those who will believe in Me through their word; that they all may be one, as You, Father, are in Me, and I in You; that they also may be one in Us, that the world may believe that You sent Me. And the glory which You gave Me I have given them, that they may be one just as We are one: I in them, and You in Me; that they may be made perfect in one, and that the world may know that You have sent Me, and have loved them as You have loved Me. "Father, I desire that they also whom You gave Me may be with Me where I am, that they may behold My glory which You have given Me; for You loved Me before the foundation of the world. O righteous Father! The world has not known You, but I have known You; and these have known that You sent Me. And I have declared to them Your name, and will declare it, that the love with which You loved Me may be in them, and I in them."

As the intensity draws the Bride closer and closer to each other and to Jesus, she will be a tangible example standing in glorious protection as a faithful witness that Her beloved is the one behind all of the events, while calling more and more to the wedding. Many will come into a saving relationship with Jesus as the most powerful prophetic anointing is poured out on His Bride. The Bible promises even the kids and the elderly will have the Spirit poured out on them in healing, miracles, manna...all in the middle of the intensity!

Joel 2:28-32 "And it shall come to pass afterward That I will pour out My Spirit on all flesh; Your sons and your daughters shall prophesy, Your old men shall dream dreams, Your young men shall see visions. And also on My menservants and on My maidservants I will pour out My Spirit in those days. "And I will show wonders in the heavens and in the earth: Blood and fire and pillars of smoke. The sun shall be turned into darkness, And the moon into blood, (this is the 6th seal!) Before the coming of the great and awesome day of the Lord . And it shall come to pass That whoever calls on the name of the Lord Shall be saved. For in Mount Zion and in Jerusalem there shall be deliverance, As the Lord has said, Among the remnant whom the Lord calls.

Tribulation is Truly Good
The fullness of those promises happen in the middle of the Great Tribulation. This should comes as no surprise to believers familiar with Jesus' teaching and Paul's writings.

John 16:33 These things I have spoken to you, that in Me you may have peace. In the world you will have tribulation; but be of good cheer, I have overcome the world."

Tribulation is a basic necessity of walking with Jesus. There is no true follower of Jesus that will not be touched by it. From the first calling of Peter until the very end of the age, every follower of Jesus has a cross to take up, a life to lay down, and a will to die to:

Matthew 16:24-27 Then Jesus said to His disciples, "If anyone desires to come after Me, let him deny himself, and take up his cross, and follow Me. For whoever desires to save his life will lose it, but whoever loses his life for My sake will find it. For what profit is it to a man if he gains the whole world, and loses his own soul? Or what will a man give in exchange for his soul? For the Son of Man will come in the glory of His Father with His angels, and then He will reward each according to his works.

The presence of tribulation in the life of a believer is a mark of truth. Jesus came to deliver mankind from the strongholds of sin and death, which the fallen world is full of. If you are being pulled from one reality into the next, if it is really happening, if the Gospel is true, then you should FEEL the transition. The uncomfortable feeling of tribulation is tangible evidence that God is giving me a new life, for real. That feeling of tribulation is the feeling of the transitioning the tempo and beat of my heart from the fallen and comfortable rhythms of a dying world to the true tune of heaven, which will never end.

God is skilled beyond measure in knowing how to precisely separate my heart alliances from the lesser false strengths of this world: money, health, security, provision. God knows how to cut the cords of trust I have attached to the physical realm so they can be reattached to God, where they always were meant to be. Tribulation is the scalpel in the master surgeon's hand:

Romans 5:3-5 And not only that, but we also glory in tribulations, knowing that tribulation produces perseverance; and perseverance, character; and character, hope. Now hope does not disappoint, because the love of God has been poured out in our hearts by the Holy Spirit who was given to us.

If Tribulation is Good, Great Tribulation is Great
Tribulation is a GOOD thing for believers, because God is the one allowing it, authorizing it, to happen. The Great Tribulation is a "great thing" for the Bride. Many times in life God allows the struggle in order to lead His people to victory (look at the story of Deborah and Barak in the Book of Judges). God allowed Job to be afflicted so that God could reveal Himself to Job. Any good parent allows some struggle to come into the lives of their kids to allow them to grow. A parent sees more and has a longer life view.

God is way more interested in me living well for trillions and trillions of years than He is about me enjoying every second of being an infant for the first 80 years. Some things you just have to work through in a process. This is the truth of life.   A lack of faith, and some historically terrible teaching, makes believers afraid of Jesus' perfectly-authored tribulation, intended to produce freedom!

A believer's fear of the tribulation would be like a believer being terrified of hell. Hell is real. People are really going there. But believers don't need to fear hell if they respond to Jesus' invitation to be safe from hell! The tribulation is no different. It is simply the consequence of resisting Jesus leadership. This is why Jesus gave us so much information about His leadership in the time of His return. The tragedy of our moment in time is that many will suffer tribulation because fear of the tribulation offended them enough to ignore all the information that would keep them from it!

The tribulation isn't some random trouble that is prophesied to engulf the world! God isn't a sloppy painter who can't keep the trouble within the lines! No! Tribulation is the BRILLIANT plan of Jesus to use the least intense means necessary to reach the greatest number of people at the deepest heart level, without ever violating free will. Period.

Jesus desires none be lost, but He won't force "anyone into that relationship with Himself, so He will "hem the whole world in" to get them to choose. This is the "valley of decision" Joel prophesied:

Joel 3:14 Multitudes, multitudes in the valley of decision! For the day of the Lord is near in the valley of decision.

This is the decision to be made: trust invisible Jesus, or trust in man-based plans to solve the intense problems that man himself has created! Out of that decision, Jesus will get a pure and spotless Bride. She will make herself ready in the time of trouble! The Bride will be releasing signs and wonders, telling the truth in the face of persecution, praying day and night for her cities and the unsaved. The cities of the Bride will be places of safety where many will run to as they come into agreement with Jesus.

In order to participate, the Bride needs to know Jesus plan and agree with it...she needs to see the wave of trouble coming and build the cities of safety by executing night and day prayer. It is this PROCESS that makes the Bride ready. This is the END of the tribulation:

Revelation 19:7 Let us be glad and rejoice and give Him glory, for the marriage of the Lamb has come, and His wife has made herself ready."

As I eluded to earlier, at the beginning of the Book of Revelation, in Chapters 2 and 3, we see seven slightly out-of-agreement churches that need adjustment and unity. This is the world we live in RIGHT NOW! Once the trouble starts in Chapter 6, the Bride progressively gets pure, spotless, and UNITED. The seven Churches become ONE Bride. This is the point of the book.

You don't need to fear the process Jesus promises to use to get a Bride when you are already engaged in being that very Bride He has committed to get. You simply need to go deeper into agreement with the process , which makes more deep in readiness!

Matthew 24:44 Therefore you also be ready, for the Son of Man is coming at an hour you do not expect.

Like any other wedding, there is so much to do! Right now there is a great deal to do to get into agreement with the wedding process Jesus has chosen. He has literally already started releasing it. The day is approaching quickly, and, like any Bride, we are responsible for many of the arrangements!

Being ready is essential because the intensity of the event will offend those not going into it with eyes wide open. Many are going to quit because they have no root. They are rooted in the comforts of a fading world system.

Planting roots in the coming kingdom by placing all of your weight, getting vision, and getting excited about the steps unfolding right now is the cure for falling away. But, this root planting has to happen before what will test the roots comes! You must begin stepping into this process before the storm comes, or the storm will pull you up. If you want to flourish in the coming years, you need to draw together with other wholehearted believers and learn to feed your heart on the superior pleasures of hearing and responding to God.

Luke 8:13 But the ones on the rock are those who, when they hear, receive the word with joy; and these have no root, who believe for a while and in time of temptation fall away.

As stated before, "falling away" means to quit being a believer. Many will fall away because they will not be ready for how intense the storm is. They haven't cared about getting their inner man, their family, their church, or their city ready for this once-in-creation transitional generation. They haven't taught themselves, or those around them, to find satisfaction in the superior pleasures of working hand in hand with God, the author and creator of everything. Many in the Church, like US if we are really honest, prefer God be an add-on to the life they desire. But people naturally desire comfort.   Comfort is the opposite of what God is calling the world into:

Luke 12:49-53 *"I came to send fire on the earth, and how I wish it were already kindled! But I have a baptism to be baptized with, and how distressed I am till it is accomplished! Do you suppose that I came to give peace on earth? I tell you, not at all, but rather division. For from now on five in one house will be divided: three against two, and two against three. Father will be divided against son and son against father, mother against daughter and daughter against mother, mother-in-law against her daughter-in-law and daughter-in-law against her mother-in-law."*

Going after comfort now does not prepare you for dealing with trouble. There is a very large wave of trouble coming. Picture a surfer out on the ocean. A surfer paddles to get in the right spot, and when the wave breaks, he rides it, has fun on it, and takes pleasure in it all the way to shore. If a surfer is in the wrong spot, the wave will crush him. Worse yet, if he is just standing in the surf zone, with his back to the wave, not paying attention, he could get really hurt or killed by the same wave he could have ridden into shore. Position matters when a wave breaks!

That is why it really matters a.) That you are standing, b.) what you are standing on, and c.) where (how deeply) you are standing right now. It is a matter of getting crushed, or having the time of your life.

This is a "once in creation" opportunity. There is only one generation of the pure and spotless Bride. She makes herself ready before the wedding. Jesus doesn't wave His hand and make her ready! No, she makes herself ready through a process. God works in processes and gives his sons and daughters space to agree with Him. He wants us "about his business." It is time to turn off all the distractions and learn to surf. But, everyone gets what they want. You have to take the first step and step away from the legitimate distractions the rest of the world celebrates. Stop sinning, for sure, but there is more to it! Stop living like things are normal when you are living in the most intense generation ever! Tear your heart and not your clothing.

Joel 2:11-13 (NLT) The Lord is at the head of the column. He leads them with a shout. This is his mighty army, and they follow his orders. The day of the Lord is an awesome, terrible thing. Who can possibly survive? Here is the answer to who can survive: That is why the Lord says, "Turn to me now, while there is time. Give me your hearts. Come with fasting, weeping, and mourning. Don't tear your clothing in your grief, but tear your hearts instead." Return to the Lord your God, for he is merciful and compassionate, slow to get angry and filled with unfailing love. He is eager to relent and not punish.

Joel goes on to describe how it is time for everyone to put normal life on hold and get with the program! (Joel 2:12-28 is the prescription for what to do). The last generation IS the greatest generation. The great cloud of witnesses longs to see this generation. We have been given much:

Luke 12:48 But he who did not know, yet committed things deserving of stripes, shall be beaten with few. For everyone to whom much is given, from him much will be required; and to whom much has been committed, of him they will ask the more.

Jesus has committed much into the hands of one generation. But, that means time matters, and position matters. Here comes the wave!! Jesus is sending a wave of glory for our pleasure, or our crushing. We are picking right now! If we are willing to change and make choices that agree with the reality of God's plans, we will forever be rewarded for those choice!

Make peace with God, now, while there is time.

T.S.

www.ingramcontent.com/pod-product-compliance
Lightning Source LLC
Chambersburg PA
CBHW061827040426
42447CB00012B/2851